CAMBRIDGE LIBRARY COLLECTION

Books of enduring scholarly value

British and Irish History, Nineteenth Century

This series comprises contemporary or near-contemporary accounts of the political, economic and social history of the British Isles during the nineteenth century. It includes material on international diplomacy and trade, labour relations and the women's movement, developments in education and social welfare, religious emancipation, the justice system, and special events including the Great Exhibition of 1851.

Gastronomy, or, The School for Good Living

The art of the chef and the appreciation of good food have been with us since time immemorial, as this work delightfully demonstrates. Dedicating the book to 'professors of culinary science in the United Kingdom', the anonymous author sets out to trace developments 'from the age of pounded acorns to the refinements of modern luxury'. The style is irresistibly extravagant, with vocabulary to match, introducing the reader to the concept of the 'theogastrophilist': one who makes his belly his god. This vividly enjoyable exploration of the pleasures of eating begins its account in ancient Greece, and then embarks on a culinary journey through European history, featuring the fourteenth-century French cook Taillevent, the recipe collection *Le viandier* that was credited to him, and John Evelyn's 1699 vegetarian treatise *Acetaria*. Of universal appeal, the work was first published in 1814, and ran to a second edition in 1822, which is reissued here.

Cambridge University Press has long been a pioneer in the reissuing of out-of-print titles from its own backlist, producing digital reprints of books that are still sought after by scholars and students but could not be reprinted economically using traditional technology. The Cambridge Library Collection extends this activity to a wider range of books which are still of importance to researchers and professionals, either for the source material they contain, or as landmarks in the history of their academic discipline.

Drawing from the world-renowned collections in the Cambridge University Library and other partner libraries, and guided by the advice of experts in each subject area, Cambridge University Press is using state-of-the-art scanning machines in its own Printing House to capture the content of each book selected for inclusion. The files are processed to give a consistently clear, crisp image, and the books finished to the high quality standard for which the Press is recognised around the world. The latest print-on-demand technology ensures that the books will remain available indefinitely, and that orders for single or multiple copies can quickly be supplied.

The Cambridge Library Collection brings back to life books of enduring scholarly value (including out-of-copyright works originally issued by other publishers) across a wide range of disciplines in the humanities and social sciences and in science and technology.

Gastronomy

or, The School for Good Living

*A Literary and Historical Essay
on the European Kitchen,
Beginning with Cadmus the Cook and King,
and Concluding with
the Union of Cookery and Chymistry*

ANONYMOUS

CAMBRIDGE
UNIVERSITY PRESS

University Printing House, Cambridge, CB2 8BS, United Kingdom

Published in the United States of America by Cambridge University Press, New York

Cambridge University Press is part of the University of Cambridge.
It furthers the University's mission by disseminating knowledge in the pursuit of
education, learning and research at the highest international levels of excellence.

www.cambridge.org
Information on this title: www.cambridge.org/9781108062886

This edition first published 1822
This digitally printed version 2013

ISBN 978-1-108-06288-6 Paperback

GASTRONOMY:

OR, THE

SCHOOL FOR GOOD LIVING;

A

LITERARY AND HISTORICAL ESSAY

ON THE

EUROPEAN KITCHEN,

BEGINNING WITH

CADMUS THE COOK AND KING, AND CONCLUDING WITH

THE UNION OF COOKERY AND CHYMISTRY.

'Αρχη και ριζα παντος αγαθȣ, η᾽ της
Γαστρος ηδονη—*Athen. Deip, l. 7. c. 5.*

Sequitur sua quemque Culina.   Juv.

SECOND EDITION.

LONDON:

HENRY COLBURN AND CO. CONDUIT STREET.

1822.

DEDICATION.

TO THE MOST ILLUSTRIOUS
AND HIGHLY DISTINGUISHED ARTISTS,
NATIONAL AND FOREIGN,
PROFESSORS OF CULINARY SCIENCE,
IN THE UNITED KINGDOM OF
GREAT BRITAIN,

HEALTH!

An enlightened age having cheered mankind with its effulgent glory, and thrown open those gastropolitechnical schools which have been closed so many thousand years, it belongs to you, most noble Seigneurs, to an-

nounce to the present age the " *commencement of a new era*,"* to exclaim
in the emphatic words of the Mantuan
Bard—

" Ultima Cumæi venit jam carminis ætas !"

It is for you to predict that Saturn
will again visit the earth, the mise-
ries of war and paper cease, and the

---

* Although this *new era* has already been announced in a famous letter some time back from
his H. R. H. the P. R. to his R. Brother, the
D. of Y. wherein he declared his resolution to
rule, " *patris virtutibus orbem* ;" yet a further
promulgation seems very advisable.

golden age return ; that there shall in future be no distinctions of seasons— the period of fruits and delicacies have no suspension—the British lion and ox meet at the same crib—the turtle lie down at the feet of the alderman.

" Incultisque rubens pendebit sentibus uva,
" Et duræ quercus sudabunt roscida mella.
Virg.

That seas of claret shall our feasts adorn,
And savoury sauces drop from every thorn.

In short, that the age of banquets has arrived, and heroes mixing with gods shall meet at the same board, and unite to form one splendid table.— May the spindles thus for ever move !

The education of our youth destined to effect this glorious change in the mundane system is confided, most noble Seigneurs, to your direction ; but as the studies of the laboratory and the practical business of your profession afford you little leisure to handle the pen, I have ventured, without being a member of your learned academy, to undertake this necessary office.

It is, however, with all due humility and deference, that I present you with this Literary and Historical Essay, expressly written to convey to your pupils just ideas of their divine origin, and the high sources from which their professional science is drawn.

Most noble Seigneurs, if this humble attempt prove congenial to your tastes; if you, who are the only competent judges, shall be satisfied of its merit, I shall feel that neither our labour nor our time has been misapplied. At all events, noble Seigneurs, I rejoice at the opportunity now afforded me of expressing my unbounded regard for you as a Body, my gratitude for the many favours you have conferred upon me, the hours of amusement you have contributed to bestow, and the many moments of extatic delight for which I am entirely indebted to your talents. With this humble testimony of my homage, I have the honour to be,

Most noble Seigneurs,

your most devoted,

grateful,

and obliged Servant,

THE AUTHOR.

PREFACE.

IT is a part of history no less curious than interesting, to observe the rise and progress of alimentary science, tracing it from the age of pounded acorns to the refinements of modern luxury. The result of this survey cannot fail to impress upon the mind one great and obvious truth; that the kitchen is the source of all the arts, that it is the prolific fountain whose savoury streams have watered the tree of knowledge, and fed it to luxuriant growth. Until the barren field was cheered by the genial rays of culinary refulgence, genius slumbered in his native clay, and talent had no birth: the canvass never started forth a living

b

man, nor Parian marble breathed an animated bust ; the mint of fancy never issued its golden coin, nor the imagination of the bard glowed with poetic fire.

" Nam si Virgilio puer, et tolerabile desit
" Hospitium, caderent omnes a crinibus Hydri."
Juv. Sat. 7.*

It is to the noble university then of pots and pans that we are indebted for all the pleasures of taste, whether they come to us in the seducing form of a finished picture, or in the more tangible exhibition of an exquisite pattée.

Under these circumstances it is natural to suppose that the professors of culinary art must have always been held in great estimation, and ranked high in society. Nor are we disap-

---

* Had Virgil been life's decent joys denied,
His bays had wither'd, and his fancy died.

pointed in this expectation. The archmagirist, whom we may consider as the chancellor of his university, has, it is true, never been invested with the gown and hood of a doctor, but he has every where his distinguishing costume. His students and his profession are both liberal ; he is acquainted with the virtues of every esculent plant : anatomy, chymistry, natural history, and philosophy ; the expansive power of heat, the rise of vapours, and the force of steam, all come within the range of his erudition. He is universally courted for his intelligence, and admired for his skill ; he is in fact the prime minister of the house. His bills are read with interest by every member ; his levees are crowded with purveyors and contractors ; numbers solicit him for *loaves and fishes* ; the greedy are enslaved by his power, and the wavering confirmed by his eloquence. He gives dinners, he entertains embassadors, he receives presents, and dispatches messengers ; and notwithstanding his peculations are often considerable, and his perquisites never trifling, he seldom retires from service without a pension.

It is then a subject of much regret that historians should have been principally employed in sounding the praises of generals, who are no better than the destroyers of mankind, and have been totally silent respecting cooks and gastrologers, who are the true Ποιμενες λαων, the shepherds and preservers of a people ; they are the worthies who have added thousands to the population of their countries ; their arms have never been raised to let loose the streams of human life, but to

give them new vigour ; they are the
physicians whose kitchen physic has
given health to the infirm. It is our
pleasant task to record their names ; to
rescue their talents and their fame from
that obscurity to which the ingratitude
of poets and historians has long consigned them.

At the same time, however, that the
kitchen has been the great patron of
the arts, and the regenerator of the
human species, justice must acknowledge that it has occasionally been the
source of some mischief. Indiscretion
may convert the greatest blessing into
evil.

" Sunt certi denique fines
" Quos ultrà citàque nequit consistere rectum."
HORACE.

We accordingly find amongst the
adorers of the kitchen a sect of fanatics,
who, losing sight of all sober Theogastro-

philism, have made those altars, which
ought only to smoke for the benefit of
man, become instrumental to his ruin.
They have not only mutilated their
own bodies in the holy fane, but they
have let loose the gout, the stone, and
the rheumatism ; vultures that gnaw
the liver, and furies that rack the
joints, in the wildness of their mad devotion. Nevertheless, we must not
condemn under one sweeping censure
the followers of this divine worship,
merely for the rage of a single sect.
The purest religion is doomed to
schism ; the just and impartial ob-
server will, therefore, make due distinction between the Theogastrophilist,
and the extravagant fervors of, what
shall I call him, the Theogastrophilofanatic. The first is mild, social, and
tolerant ; the latter, bigoted, proud,
and cruel. His desires know no

bounds ; his appetite is insatiable ; he
stirs up nation against nation, and
brother against brother. Every thing
must bow down before his idol ; seas
that give the most abundant fish,
islands that produce the most fragrant
perfumes, and the finest spices ; countries that yield the choicest fruits and
the most delicious wines are all ransacked for offerings at his shrine.—
Nay, such is his avidity, that navies
have been launched, and armies sent
forth ; treasures spent, and rivers of
blood made to flow, for the acquisition
of a salted cod or a pickled herring, a
hogshead of sugar and a puncheon of
rum. Such melancholy details the
history of culinary science will occasionally present. But we will not
dwell upon the unfavourable parts of
the picture. We will turn away from
these disgusting scenes, and contem-

plate the kitchen as it really is, a benefit to mankind, the source of pleasure, the promoter of society, the
cheerful friend that reconciles the dif-
ferences of contending parties, restores
good humour, cheers and animates the
hungry and expecting guest, stops
even the barking mouth of the cynic,
and gives to acrimony itself the smiles
of benevolence.

In the little Essay which the author
now offers to the public, he certainly
has some apology to make for a few
compounds,* as well as the imperfect
manner in which he has sketched so

---

* When an eminent journalist called the speech
of the French Empress to the Senate a *femino-
masculine* address, the author trusts that the com-
pound of Theogastrophilofanatic, and other
"*sesquepedalia verba,*" will be received as perfectly
legitimate. It is by compounds that languages
become copious and expressive; several roots

vast a field of science. He has, however, endeavoured to be as lively as the
grave subject of history will admit.—
If his table be served agreeable to
public taste, and the manner in which
he has dressed his materials approved,
his magazine is not exhausted; his
larder can afford considerable delicacies, yet untouched; and he can present some stores which, with good
sauce, will offer at least variety to the
literary Gourmand. The readers may
rely upon the author's testimony, that
he presents no unwholesome diet, no
poison under a specious shew of morality, and that he draws from many
sources, what even pedagogues will not
despise. In short, he proposes to give

---

combined in one word give that word a triple and
quadruple force. The use of compounds should
never therefore be checked.

all those elementary books, which, in
concert with the politechnical schools
at Paris, and the *Jury of Legitimation*
in the *Champs Elyseés*,* will form a
complete course of Gastrology.

---

* This is the name of a well known promenade
at Paris, near the ntrance of which is situated the
magnificent palace of the Author of *l' Almanach des
Gourmands*. In this palace is established that
August Tribunal, known by the name of *Jury of
Legiti nation*. There is comfirmed without appeal, the merit and legitimacy of every piece destined to appear on the alimentary stage. There,
the patents of preference are granted, the stars of
culinary honors distributed. All the world at
London sighs for the establishment of a similar
tribunal. How long, O metropolis of England,
" *quousque*," how long will you continue to envy
your Gallic rival! But what may we not hope?
I will say to you, as an elegant and classical Prince
said to the most distinguished General of this age,

" Nil desperandum Teucris, duce et auspice
    Teucro." *Hor:*

GLOSSARY.

AGREEABLE to the rules of every writer on subjects of science, it has been found necessary to introduce into the present work, a little hellenized English, that our ideas might not be cramped by an imperfect phraseology. The unlearned reader is, therefore, humbly presented with the annexed Glossary. We do not presume to offer to the scholar etymologies or explanations, which to him would be superfluous.

Adephagus, Great Eater.

Agrinomy, Precepts for Field Culture.

Archmagirist, Chief Cook.

Buphagus, Beef-eater.

Gastrology, Science of Eating.

Gastronomy, Precepts for Eating.

Gastrophilism, the Love of Eating.

Gastrophilist, One who loves Eating.

Gastropolitechnical, the various arts for the gratification of the Belly.

Gastrophilanthropic, the Benevolent Purveyor for the Belly of others.

Magirist, a Cook.

Magirological, what treats of Cooks.

Ænology, the Science of Wines.

Opsology, the Science of Condiments.

Opsartytical, the Culinary Art.

Theogastrophilism, Belly Worship.

Theogastrophilist, One who makes his Belly his God.

Theogastrophilofanatic, One who runs into extravagant fervours in his Belly Worship.

THE SCHOOL

GOOD LIVING.

ORPHEUS,* by the sweetness of his
voice and the enchanting tones of his
lyre, drew men and herds around him,
and melted even flinty rocks to soft-
ness.† Amphion also, by the harmonious sounds of music, built the walls
of Thebes. Melody has therefore done
wonders. But after all, the delightful

---

* Saxa ferasque lyrâ movit Rhodopeius Orpheus.
Ovid Met.

† Dictus et Amphion Thebanæ conditor arcis
Saxa movere sono testudinis, et prece blandâ
Ducere quo vellet. *Hor. Art. Poet.*

B

notes of the ten-stringed instruments,
the cymbals or the flute, will do nothing towards the support of animal
life ; and even the most abstemious
disciples of Pythagoras have, in this
respect, considered them in no other
light than slender diet. When mankind, therefore, became united, and
sought for shelter and protection in
towns and cities,* it was necessary to
provide for their subsistence, and teach
them the great ties of social life.

It originally happened, then, that
Cadmus, archmagirist † to the king of

---

* Oppida cœperunt munire, et ponere leges.

Hor. lib. 1, *Sat.* 3.

† Archmagirist signifies chief cook ; it is derived from 'Αρχιμάγειρον. Juvenal mentions this
officer—

Finxerunt pariter librarius, archimagiri.

Sat. 9, *v.* 109.

Sidon, and in whose veins flowed the
purest blood of Olympus, tired of
being the chief purveyor to the palate
of a single prince, aspired at becoming
the general caterer and foster-father of
mankind. And as he had not tied on
the culinary apron, armed his side with
the large knife, girded his loins with
the formidable steel, or adorned his
head with the white cap, exhibited
himself, in short, in all the insignia of
his office,* without having previously
taken the degree of master of arts,
doctor of physic, law, divinity, astro-
nomy, music, and geometry, no one
was better qualified to insure the success of this great undertaking. Having once made up his mind to the
project, Cadmus took his departure

---

* Athen. Deipn. lib. vii., c. xi., p. 291.

from the kitchens of his royal master, and quitted, not without tears of regret, the scenes of all his former pleasures. But where was he to bend his steps? how forward the objects which he had in view? Having learnt the unproductive prodigies of Orpheus and Amphion, and being assured that these divine harmonists had left their hearers with craving stomachs and empty mouths, he resolved to unfold the page of science, and to instruct the understandings of the Greeks, a people whom he suspected had dispositions by no means averse to good living. He thought it high time that they should be taught to renounce the use of crude vegetables and raw meat; a diet only fit for the uncivilized hunter of the forest, or the barbarous and wandering tribes of Scythia, and by no means in character with the stationary and quiet inhabitants of a populous city.

Orpheus had *touched upon this string*,* but he might as well have preached in a wilderness.

With the office of archmagirist was combined another of higher distinction. No victim at Sidon was ever sacrificed but by the hand of the king's Grans Queux † of the kitchen. Cadmus was, from his official situation, present at every ceremony of this kind,

---

* Sylvestres homines sacer, interpresque deorum,
Cædibus et victu fœdo deterruit Orpheus.

Hor. Art. Poet.

* The Grans Queux was an officer of considerable dignity in the palaces of princes; all the others were subservient to him. The list may be seen, Lib. Nig. ed. 4, p. 347.

and initiated in all the mysteries of religion, as well as the delicate manner of seasoning the meats to be served at the banquets of the gods. The same sacred volume, containing the ceremonial to be observed in offering up the productions of the earth at their altars, explained also the best methods of rendering them savoury to the smell and delicious to the taste, a circumstance of which the religious devotees never failed to profit.

Being thus intimately acquainted with this book of divine worship and opsology, Cadmus embarked on his expedition into Greece. As he was the grandson of Neptune, he took the opportunity of paying a visit by the way to many of his marine relations. Each received him with due distinction; and all were eager to serve his

table with the best sample of their
stores. Nor was their hospitality
lightly regarded. He was not of a
disposition to let a good dish pass by
unnoticed. Thus doubly armed then
for the business of the kitchen, he arrived at Thebes. Since the departure
of the lyric musicians, the inhabitants
of that famous city had hung their
heads in a kind of silent despair, each
regarding with horror the denouement
of a piece, which, without the inter-
vention of some deity, seemed to promise little more than that of leaving
the actors the miserable alternative of
either dying of hunger, or feeding upon
each other.

Cadmus, on quitting Sidon, carried
off with him a celebrated flute player
belonging to the king's orchestra,

called Harmonia,* which, by some
means or other, has been since changed into Hermione. With such a com-
panion he won all hearts, and conci-
liated all dispositions ; but, in order to
effect a perfect understanding amongst
his audience, it was necessary that the
belly should be in unison with the
head and heart. " For a hungry belly,"
says the proverb, " has no ears."—
The great difficulty, however, was to
make it hear reason, and make it wait
patiently for the hour of repast. Our
literary cook had no other expedient
to console the Thebans, and to keep
up their spirits, than that of teaching
them the alphabet.† They thus got

---

* Athen. Deipn. l. xiv., c. 22., p. 658.

† Plin. Nat. Hist. lib. vii., c. 56.

Exclusive of the solid benefits which Cadmus

a glimpse (though, it must be acknow-
ledged, with difficulty,) of the possi-
bilities of tasting some pleasure, and
finding some amusement, in the intervals of their meals.

From the very first banquet, Cadmus had given no bad specimen of his
talent, so that they soon began to discover the sort of man they had to deal
with, and the kind of stuff of which he
was made : but he quickly had it in
his power to shew his foster children,
that he equally possessed the talent of

---

procured for the Grecians, by teaching them the
culinary arts and letters, they were also indebted
to him for the invention of writing. This was
first taught in the way called Βȣϛροφηδον, where the
first line runs from left to right, and the next from
right to left, and had its appellation from the
manner in which the ploughman turns his
steers.

preparing a banquet for the inhabitants of heaven as for the tenants of earth.

The continual journeys in which Cadmus had been engaged, had hitherto prevented the celebration of his marriage with Hermione. As this young beauty was the daughter of Mars and Venus, and scrupulously virtuous withal, he had encountered many difficulties on his route, by which the accomplishment of his wishes had been retarded. In the mean time, until a more favourable state of affairs should present themselves, she retired under the protection of Electra the Chaste,* where she was discovered by her mother under the assumed name of Peisinöe,† and who, with the assist-

---

* Soph. Trag. Electra.

† Peisinöe, derived from πειθειν and νῦς, signifying persuasion.

ance of her friend Mercury,* soon arranged every thing to the full content
of the contracting parties.

The marriage being thus happily
consummated, the bridegroom resolved
to regale both his own and his wife's
divine relations. He accordingly sent
a very polite request, that they would
all repair to Thebes, and do him the
hon'or to taste his soups. No sooner
had the cards of invitation reached
Olympus, where the gods were sitting
in full council, than they, sensible of
the talents of their host, hastened the
preparations for their descent, each
with his pockets well lined with presents † for the new-married couple.

---

* Mercury, or eloquence.

† Nonn. Dionys. lib. v.—Euripides also notices
this visit of the gods to celebrate the nuptials of

The arrival of such a concourse of di-
vinities created some alarm, lest the
gates of the city should be choked up
with their retinues ; orders were therefore immediately issued, that seven
other gates should be thrown open,
upon each of which, according to the
direction in which it stood, was the
name of a planet.

Never was there a fête more brilliant ; never was there banquet more
handsomely served ; never did the harmony of sounds exert herself with
more energy to bear away the palm
from the harmony of culinary art.
The first called to her aid the Muses,

Hermione, when Amphion raised the walls of
Thebes with his harp.

'Αρμονιας δε ποτ' εις υμεναιους
'Ηλυθον Ουρανιδοι, φερμιγχι τετειχεα Θηβας
Τας Αμφιονας τελυρας, &c.

who had for once consented to be present at the entertainment, and where
each played her part to admiration.
Apollo, however, did not fail to per-
ceive that the nine sisters did not produce that effect for which they were
eminently qualified. It was evident
that the guests were so deeply engaged with the harmony of the culinary art, that they scarcely took their
eyes off the table. He, therefore, resolved to join the nine sisters; but
vain was the attempt to attract the
notice of the company, for all the
gods, in a moment of enthusiastic rapture, arose with one accord, and confirmed to Cadmus the title of the Great
Preserver of Universal Harmony.*

---

* Jupiter had before bestowed on Cadmus
this title, when by his assistance the God of

In the mean time, the Thebans considered as angels those who thus daily

---

Thunder recovered the bolt which Typhon had
stolen from him. " Sing," said the Father of
the Gods to Cadmus, (after that Pan, who was
constitutionally of a timid disposition, and who
had no inclination to encounter Typhon, had
given to Cadmus his pipe and his cloven feet,)
" sing of peace, and serenity shall be restored to
the heavens ; become a shepherd but for one day,
that this pastoral pipe may restore liberty to the
shepherd of the world, and thy services shall not
pass without recompence ; thou shalt become
the great preserver of the harmony of the uni-
verse, and the beautiful Harmony shall be thy
wife—

> Ego ibi digna laboribus
> Dabo duplicia munera.

Te enim salvatorem perficiam, Harmoniæ mundi,
et Harmoniæ conjugem."

What a variety of interesting events, which
took place in the journeys of Cadmus and Hermione, are we obliged to pass over in silence ?

contributed to their good living. They
never quitted their presence but with
regret, or came near their dwelling
but with an anxious wish to catch
their ear. Whilst they were thus occupied in obtaining culinary science,
all other seemed but as a feather in the
scale. They gave themselves up so
entirely to the subject, that it was not
long before they began to find out that
there were some dishes, which no

The obligation would be great to any writer who
might give a complete history of this cooking
king to the world, one whom we may boldly call
the king of cooks. I know that his history is
obscured by many difficulties, and more so, because every mythologist will have his god to have
been a cook. But this ought not to deter the
literary gastrophilist, anxious to make known the
origin of that divine art, which is the true source
of all the joys and all the pleasures of human
life.

powers of stomach could render nu-
tritious, nor the best gastric juices
themselves concoct.* They made
such frequent and heavy complaints to
Cadmus on this subject, that, sensible
of their griefs, and touched by their
noble perseverance in fulfilling with
so much courage their manducatory
functions, he determined to move
heaven and earth to obtain for his convivial pupils a better digestion, and,
cost what it would, to procure for
them this additional benefit.

His daughter Semele was on the
point of being married. Jupiter, long

---

* They seemed to have been reduced to that
distressing situation which Horace so well de-
scribes when he says,
Dulcia se in bilem vertent, stomachoque tu-
    multum
Lenta feret pituita.

in the habit of casting his eye upon terrestrial beauties, had not lost sight of her. He had, besides, one day the good fortune to get a peep at her when bathing; and well instructed in all matters that were proceeding here below, he shortly after transported himself to the habitation of this young beauty.* To promise her every thing she asked, and obtain her hand, was but the business of a few days; and the father of the gods, without the

* This account of Cadmus, Semele, and the birth of Bacchus, is taken, *mutatis mutandis*, from a publication of M. Dupuis, professor of rhetoric at the college of Lizieux, &c. A great part of it may be found in the Encyclopedia Methodique, art. Bacchus. Nonnus appears to have been the guide of M. Dupuis. *Vide Non. Dionys.* lib. v.

least scruple, took to wife the daughter
of a cook.

We know that many attempts have
been made to gloss over this marriage
—but, leaving it to the ecclesiastical
court to pronounce respecting its legitimacy, we shall simply state that Semele,* when she was seven months
gone with child, upon an occasion of
one of those longings which women
in that state are known to possess,
took a fancy to amuse herself with one
of her husband's firebrands, as she had
often done with those of her father;
but she learnt, alas! too late, that to
handle the fire of heaven was no
child's play, as in a single moment she
was reduced to ashes.†

* Ovid. Met., lib. iii , v. 301.
†   ——donisque jugalibus arsit.
                                        Ovid. Met.

Jupiter and his son Sebasius * were fortunately at hand, and with no little difficulty were enabled to save her child.

As it was never expected that the infant should have seen the day so soon, there was no pap ready for him, and no cradle or child linen prepared ; and besides, to have obtained his full growth, he ought to have remained two months longer in his mother's womb.

The father of the gods, therefore,

---

* This son of Jupiter seems to arrive upon this occasion a day after the fair. Indeed, it appears as if it were the only exploit in which he had ever engaged. The false Orpheus is, I believe, the only author who has ever brought him upon the classic stage. There is, indeed, a Sebasius mentioned in the *Golden Ass* of Apuleius, but that cannot be our hero.

called to mind an operation,* which
he had seen performed with great success by his father-in-law; and instantly
made a kind of slanting cut in his
thigh, where he deposited the young
gentleman, not without some risk of
his suffocation.

From this bond of divine union,
Bacchus sprung to life. He soon,
however, shewed himself to be a spoilt
child, and made the juice of the vine
absolutely flow in rivers amongst the

---

* The operation to which Jupiter referred was
probably that of crimping a fish, or cutting up
some animal for the spit, or, perhaps, serving up
a pudding in a pike's belly. We cannot exactly
ascertain which of these might have occurred.

Imperfectus adhuc infans genetricis ab alvo
Eripitur, patrioque tener (si credere dignum)
Insuitur femori, maternaque tempora complet.
                              Ovid. Met., lib. iii.

inhabitants of his native city. But
the new liquor mounted so terribly
into their heads, that their descendants
have always been in some degree af-
fected by it. The Greeks have reproached them for their stupidity,*
but never in the presence of Hercules
the Theban, who would have dealt
pretty roundly with them had they
dared to take such a liberty. Strangers
also stood equally in awe of this beef-
eating god,† and had the same discre-

---

* This stupidity of the Thebans became quite
proverbial, and obtained for them the ancient re-
proach of Bœotian hogs. Thus in Horace,

Bœotùm in crasso jurares aëre natum.

† Hercules was called Buphagus, a word derived from Βὖς and φαγειν. He being accused of
carrying off the ox of a countryman, and having
eaten him whole for his breakfast. It has also been
said that he had three rows of teeth. He got the
name of Adephagus to express his appetite.

tion as the Greeks; but after his death, all the world openly declared, that the great capacity of the Bœotian stomachs had done considerable injury to their heads.

During the ages when the hands of royal wives did not disdain to knead the meal, and the hands of royal husbands to roast the meat;* during those

---

* Abraham, who was a king and a shepherd, we are told, " entered hastily into the tent of Sarah, and said, make ready quickly three measures of fine meal, and knead it, and make cakes upon the hearth." The Roman ladies also made bread for their families; and the heroes of Homer would rather have renounced the siege of Troy, than have submitted the duties of the spit to the hands of subalterns. If some of our modern ladies acquired a few of these solid accomplishments, instead of torturing the strings of a piano, they might not make worse wives, or be less able to amuse their husbands.

ages, for ever to be celebrated, when
their little princely offspring contended
with each other for the honor of turn-
ing the spit, and basting the meat, the
art of cooking made little progress.
But with respect to war, it was far
otherwise : rather by address than by
force, the genius of the blood-stained
plain, insensibly as it were, drew the
spit from the hands of kings, and in-
sinuated the sword into its place. It
is more than probable, however, that
this great business would never have
terminated so prosperously, had it not
been for that great undertaking of
Epeus.* No one, indeed, was a better
judge of the *piercing* merit of the spit,

* For an account of this hero, see the notes of
Ruæus in the Delphin edition of Virgil, lib. ii.,
Æn. See also Varro, lib. vi.

than this great engineer of the Grecian
army before Troy ; and the condescension of this warrior, who was the cook
of his legion,* would have been inex-
cusable, and indeed inexplicable, but
for those circumstances which occasioned it. Wielding with equal dex-
terity the chisel of the carpenter and
the cleaver of the cook, he constructed
that famous horse so fatal to proud
Ilium ; and when he came to *stuff* it
with soldiers, he found it necessary to
arm them with short swords, to which
he gave the name of *couteau* † or *cutlass ;* and at the same time, by an ac-

---

* Epeum fumificum qui legione nostræ habet
coctum cibum.

† This instrument was a kind of cut and thrust.
The dirk seems to come the nearest to it in description, and was formerly used by the high-
lander to carve his venison.

commodation equally just and reason-
able, (and to which Ulysses, the great
kitchen rival of Epëus, also lent his
authority,) the long sword received the
appellation of the *spit*—a name which
it preserves even to this day; only that
Epëus differed from the modern artist,
in as much as he was not very fond of
having any dealing with it afterwards—
and *timid as Epeus* * became proverbial.

This first advantage gained by the
military over the devotees of the kitchen, it only remained for them to
display the ensigns of their victory ;
and, consequently, kings and princes
armed themselves with the *cutlass*.
Many, however, after the example of
Achilles † would never abandon the

---

* Erasm. Adag.   † Hom. Il.

noble custom of making use of it as usual, to carve their meat with their own hands : and even to the present day, there are many great potentates who shew no great disinclination to amuse themselves in the same way.

In the mean time, war began to absorb entirely the time of princes, and kept them altogether alienated from the business of the kitchen ; but still, as if they felt how seriously its affairs concerned the great objects of life, they only consigned them to those in whom they could place the fullest confidence.

It has been remarked, but, perhaps, with a considerable seasoning of malice, that both prince and people owe many blessings to this cause.

The greater the waste that war made upon human life, the greater were the efforts of the kitchen to supply the deficiency. For she shewed no evil disposition to her antagonist in this respect, but readily offered her aid to those whom fire and sword had condescended to spare.

Science however, always averse from war, could not long remain in a country of barbarians, who seemed to despise the charms of peace; she, therefore, fled from the sanguinary plains of Bœotia, and bore away with her those elementary books, and receipts of the culinary art, which Cadmus had inintroduced amongst her sons.

The North, inhabited by a people, who, like the Thracians,* had a sove-

---

* See Ælian, lib. viii., c. vi. "Ex veteribus Thracibus neminem aiunt literas novisse, imo turpissimum putarunt et summum dedecus inhabitantes Europam Barbaris literis uti."

reign contempt for literature, drove back this pacific caravan. There was then no alternative but to look southward; and accordingly, by *forced marches*, the corps reached Athens, which had already began to call loudly for their presence, and to wait their arrival with inexpressible impatience. Happily for the Thessalians, but unhappily for the Greeks, their cavalry picked up a few stragglers from the company; under the guidance of whose talents the luxury of the Thessalian table soon spread in a manner which induced Darius to pay them a visit, as the figs * of Athens afterwards allured Xerxes.

---

* The Attic soil abounded in figs. Some demagogue procured a law to forbid their exportation merely to gratify the people, at the expense of the land-owner. This gave rise to a numerous

It would be difficult to decide whether the philosopher or the culinary artist was most cherished by the Athenians; but upon this we may rely, that all books upon gastrological subjects were so greedily devoured by them, and multiplied so rapidly in their hands, that the library of *the Great King* * himself would not have contained their number.

The distinctions likewise which the officers of the kitchen enjoyed must not be passed by unnoticed. To their magirists was given an appointment

race of unprincipled informers, who got the name of sycophants: they courted the populace at the expense of truth and justice. Thus the original fig denouncer, has been applied to every mean fawne .—*Athen.*, p. 74.

* The title of the Great King.

('Αναξ ὁ μέγαλος), was one which the Greeks bestowed on the King of Persia.

of culinary artists,* who presided at
all public occasions, when the people
were enjoined to assist them. To their
magirists were deputed the right of
presiding at the sacrifices, of making
libations, and performing the marriage
ceremonies. To them also was en-
trusted the business of arranging, cutting up and dressing the animals that
had been immolated. To them also
was given the office of herald,† by
which they were empowered to confirm
the oaths of treaties over the victims
they had slaughtered, in the exercise
of which function they took the name
of Ceryces‡.

---

* Athen. l. xiv., c. xxiii., p. 660.

† Athen. l. xiv., c. xxii.

‡ Ceryces from Ceryx, whence the heralds were
called κηρυκες.

'Εκlως δὲ προτι ἄςυ δύο κήρυκας 'επεμπε
Καρπαλίμως ἄρνας τε φέρειν.   Hom. Il.

There is one remarkable circumstance, which, as it confers infinite
honour on the kitchen, ought not to
be omitted. It is, that whilst a salary
was assigned to the herald, we no
where find that the cook ever received
the smallest remuneration for his services.—What noble disinterestedness !
what honorable employment ! what
distinguished liberality ! To the culinary ministers alone was it granted to
live upon the applauses which a grateful country lavished upon them ; to
have the glory of standing forth the
free and gratuitous fathers of the
people.—No salary ! no perquisite ! no
sale of offices ! no kitchen grease ! no
cheese parings nor candle-ends !!*—

---

* If this passage should ever meet the eye of
any of his Majesty's ministers, or the Indian di-

O noble magirists! how must the ministers of modern states blush in contemplating so pure a system of administration!—From your mouths issued sentiments which none but you could have dared to utter*—" We, we," you exclaimed, " are the only mortals to whose prayers the gods have listened ; to us they have confided the true secret of rendering human life completely happy."

As the taste of the Athenians gradually grew more and more refined, they lost sight of that primitive frugality in their repasts which had hitherto been proverbial. No longer content with heaping favors on who-

---

rectors, the author trusts that the principle it conveys will not be lost upon them.

 * Athen. Deipn. lib. xiv., ch. xxiii.

ever had procured some new source of
aliment for their country, they extended their gratitude for every fresh
delight of the palate, without any regard to prudence, and bestowed the
rights of citizenship even on the children of its author.   How many kings,
and how many consuls, vied with each
other in doing homage to the sons of
Chæorephilus,* in consideration of
their father's merits, who first introduced the use of salted meats into
their city.

Some few gastrologists and gastro-
nomists, it must be allowed, were so
intoxicated with the success of culinary science, that they lost their heads,
and literally abandoned the bright and
cheering *luminary* of the kitchen for

---

* Athen. lib. iii., c. xxiii., p. 119.

the *luminaries of heaven;* and made a
most singular division of their time,
by spending the day in seeking for
noon at two o'clock, and by wearing
out the night in baying at the moon.
These deserters of the art were esteem
ed *lunatics* by many, but, agreeable to
the new vocation which they exer-
cised, assumed the titles of *Astrolo-
gers* and *Astronomers*, instead of *Gastrologers* and *Gastronomers*. They
were, however, most cruelly mortified
to find that they made few proselytes.
There were amongst others, two things
which they could not comprehend,
and which, indeed, to them was a pro-
blem difficult to be solved. It was,
on the one hand, the ardour with which
mankind threw themselves upon terrestrial kids, goats, bucks, and bulls;
and again, on the other, the extraor-

dinary indifference they shewed for
these animals when translated into the
celestial plains.

From the very first appearance of
magirology in Greece, it produced ef-
fects absolutely magical ; it civilized
the people, it cherished the arts, it
perfected the taste, it taught in what
the first good, the *summum bonum* of
life, consisted ; it made the works of
genius to be idolized.

It was shortly received as the worship of the Magi in the East, and as
quickly instructed its disciples there,
as in Egypt, in all the virtues of the
most concealed esculent plants. Thanks
to it also, as if by some supernatural
power, Greece, so vain of her Seven
Wise Men, became now proud of her
" Seven Sages of the Kitchen ;"* and

·* Athen. Deipn. lib. ix., c. 5.

posterity has confirmed her judgment.

In fact, the names of the first are
now scarcely remembered; the detail
of their mental feasts little known;
their works lost to the world, and the
wisdom of their laws disregarded. Those
precepts which were circulated with so
much pomp and such literary triumph, exist now only by tradition,
while the names of the latter are
echoed from tongue to tongue; their
rules daily observed; their composi-
tions ever admired; and their laws
universally established, and scrupulously obeyed. And who now,
without blushing up to the eyes,
would venture to acknowledge his ignorance, that Agris * of Rhodes was
the first who taught the true method

* Athen. Deipn. lib. viii. c. 5. p. 379.

of dressing fish? that it was *Nereus*, of Chios, who made the conger a dish for the gods: that it was *Orion* who invented la sauce blanche; and Chariades la sauce blonde; that Lampriadas discovered the merits of la sauce noire; that Atlantus formed the most perfect restorative, and that Euthynus prepared legumes with such perfect art, that he was named *Lentillus?*

Sublime geniuses!—Mortal ministers of the immortal Adephagia! pardon the feeble homage which I render to your memories! If I have ventured to mention your illustrious names, it is only to favour some young gastrophilists, who may have had the misfortune to be reared by nurses so negligent, that they have omitted to engrave sufficiently your profound merit upon their tender minds.

As when the rosy-fingered goddess,*
rising from Tithonus saffron bed,
awakes the busy swarms of Hymettus,
they, jealous to dispute with the first
rays of the Sun and the morning
breath of the Zephyr, the pearly dew-
drops which bespangle the flowers,
quit with eager flight their mountain

---

* The author trusts that he shall not be visited
with severe criticism for this simile, as over-
charged with poetic images for a prosaic history.
It is his wish to carry on his readers without fatigue,
and to present them with as many fine prospects as
the country through which he has to conduct them
will afford. At the same time, he feels aware of
a little plagiarism, which on this, as well as on
other occasions, he is ready to acknowledge.

Qualis apes æstate novâ per florea rura,
Exercet sub sole labor, cum gentis adultos
Educunt fœtus, et cùm liquentia mella
Stipant, et dulci distendunt nectare cellas.

                                        Virg.

hives, and spread over the plains of
Attica, with no other guide than the
fragrant gales that emanate from the
bosom of the enamelled field ; so, at
the first sparkling of the newly-lighted
fires of Athens, troops of theogastrophilists * from all the country round,
greedy to get the first share of the culinary dainties which they promise,
abandon with palpitating hearts their
houses, their homes, children, and
friends, to lay siege to the city gates,
dispersing through every quarter of the
town, without other conductor than
the regaling steams which the flesh-

* *Theogastrophilists.* As this word may often
occur, we must observe, for the sake of the ladies
who may honor these pages with their fair eyes,
that it means those people whose *bellies are their
god*—a worship of great antiquity.—Vide Glossary.

pots and spits so deliciously and widely expanded.

The culinary scholars at Athens, reared under the most experienced instructors, soon spread abroad the *savoir vivre* or true knowledge of good living, and quickly made pupils who surpassed even their masters.

Syracuse, Tarentum, Sybaris, and Crotona, produced such consummate artists, and so superior to those of Greece, that, struck with their preeminence over other nations, the Athenians, instead of giving them the appellation of barbarians, were obliged to bestow upon the country in which these towns were placed, the title of *Great Greece*.

But mark, at what a refinement of wickedness those rude nations arrived, who broke down the barriers of civi-

lization. Their voracious appetites,
which even the crude flesh of horses
could scarcely satisfy, induced them
to wage war against every thing that
did not contribute to animal gratification.

Their total indifference to the cul-
tivation of the understanding made
them regardless of science, by which
alone the mind is softened and im-
proved. Being wholly immersed in
objects of sensual indulgence, and the
means of accelerating and augmenting
pleasures, they discarded every thing
in the shape of a book, or only made
use of it to light their fires.

Had they but availed themselves
of the works of mythology for such
purposes, there would have been little
to lament ; they might have destroyed

them as they did the images of the gods,
which they smashed like glass. They
might have demolished the works of
the philosophers as they did their
schools; those of jurisprudence, as
they overthrew their tribunals; those
of the grammarians, whose pupils they
enslaved; those of the poets, to whose
harmony their ears were deaf, and to
whose beauties their eyes were blind;
or those of the historians, whose long
recitals they could never digest in the
short space which intervened between
their meals. Had their overwhelming
hand been confined to these, one might
have pardoned the fault; but who will
advocate their cause, when they learn
that they had the barbarity to make
an *auto da fè* of the works of culinary
science!—subjects too which so di-

rectly came within the range of their capacity.

When we seriously reflect on this calamity, who that has a susceptible heart can refrain from melting into tears at the melancholy idea that they must go down into the grave, alas! unenlightened by so many sages who wrote for the delight of man? Science, no doubt, mourns over the loss, but the more feeling gastrophilist is plunged into a despair of grief, which not even time itself will be ever able to remove.

The privation which the world has suffered may be, in some degree, estimated by the following list of magirological writers, whose revered names have happily survived the destruction of their works.

Mithæcus,[1] on the culinary arts, ('Οψαρτυ]ικος,) who was carried off, together with his works, from a city, where nothing better issued from the kitchen than a broth as black as ink.

Parmenon[2] of Rhodes, author of precepts on cooking (Μαγειρικη διδασκαλία).

Philoxenes[3] of Cytherea, on suppers (περῖ δειπνῶν).

Actides[4] of Chios, Tyndaricus the Sicyonian, or Zoporinus, authors to whom Baton, in his comedy on Benefits, (εν ευεργέταις,) pleasantly calls celebrated and famous.

---

1. Athen. Deipn. l. vii., p. 325.
2. Athen. l. vii , c. xvii., p. 30S.
3. Id. l. iv., c. xi., p. 146.
4. Id. l. xiv., c. xxiii., p. 662.

Artemidorus,[5] on culinary art, Οψαρτυ]ικα,) a work full of invaluable receipts, if it has any resemblance to that of Mattys fortunately transmitted to posterity.

Hicesius, on alime nt (περὶ υλης).

Philotemus,[7] on culinary art (Οψαρτυ]ικα).

Mnesitheus[8] of Athens, on good things to eat (περῖ εδεςῶν).

Heraclides[9] of Cumænus, on the preparations for a feast (παρασκευαςικον).

Heraclides[10] *of Tarentum,* on the banquet (συμιποσια).

---

5. Athen. Deipn. l. xiv., p. 662.
6. Ib. lib. vii., c. xi., p. 294.
7. Ib. ib. c. xvii., p. 309.
8. Id. l. ii., c. xiii., p. 54.
9. Id. l. iv., c. x., p. 145.
10. Id. l. iii., c. 33., p. 120.

Philoxenus,[11] Numenius Heracle-
otes, Metreas Pitanæus, Hegemon
Thasius, surnamed the little Lentillus,
and all those stores of culinary science
which form the collection under the
title of *Opsartuticos*, we have to deplore ; and amongst others the writings
of, *Acesias*,[12] *Acestius*, *Agis*, *Criton*,
Diocles, *Enthydemus* of Athens, *He-
gesippus* of Tarentum, *Stephanus ;
Pantalon*,[13] *Simonactides* of Chios ;
Mnaseas ;[14] *Architas*[15] *Harmonicus*,
Sophron, and *Dionysius*, as well as
the emphatic verses of Timachidas
of Rhodes, or the golden numbers of,

---

11. Athen. Deipn. lib. i., c. iii., p. 5.
12. Athen. l. xii., c. 13., p. 1516.
13. Poll. Œnom.
14. Columell. l. xii., c. iv.
15. Athen. l. xii., c. xiii., p. 156.

Archestratus[16] on Gastronomy, the very Homer of the kitchen.

Nor did the Barbarians treat the culinary classics of the Romans better than those of the Greeks ; even the smallness of their number could not save them from that persecution which annihilated every thing that did not contribute to the maw. They gave no quarter to M. Ambius,* to Manas Licinius, nor even to C. Matius, a Roman knight, the friend of Cæsar and of Cicero—men who occupied themselves in giving rules for the establisment of bakers and cooks, traiteurs and purveyors worthy of a city, which had become the metropolis of the world, and the center of good living.

---

16. Athen. l. i., c. iii., p. 4.

* Columell. l. xii., ch. iv.

Who would believe that even the treatise of Apicius *de irritamentis Gulæ*
found no one to defend it ? and, but
for the devotion of some charitable
souls, we should have had to deplore
the loss of the little Dispensary of
Cælius Apicius *de arte coquinariá.**

Peace to your shades, ye noble magirologists ! Farewel, ye warm and
philanthropic patrons of the hungry !
How gloriously were your lives consecrated to the benefit of mankind !
How nobly were your talents employed ! How vast your labours, and in-

---

* One cannot help being surprized that the
French have never published a translation of this
work. Lister, a physician in Queen Anne's reign,
gave an excellent Latin edition of it, with a very
curious and learned preface, containing a list of
all the medical men who had ever written on the
art of dressing food.

defatigable your industry, in succour-
ing the needy, administering to the
distresses, and relieving the wants of a
gaping generation ! Posterity is just
to your virtues.—In the scattered
fragments of your rich opsology, we
trace with delight the delicacy of your
taste, the transcendant powers of your
invention, and the happy application
of your consummate genius !

As the first man of letters in Greece
was a cook, it is natural for the language which he taught to have bor-
rowed its energy from his art. And
this is curiously the fact: for we cannot
but remark how much the Greek
writers are indebted to the kitchen for
all their most ardent expressions ; for
the fire and vigour of their diction.
Read but Pindar the Theban, who
sung with such excellence those heroes

D

that distinguished themselves at the
Olympic games ;* and you will find
that his muse is more exalted, more
fraught with poetic fire, more vehe-
ment and rapid in its course, in pro-
portion as he has drawn from that ela-
borate and effulgent source.† Nor is
it surprizing, when we reflect that the
first man who bore away the prize at

---

* Sive quos Elea domum reducit
  Palma cœlestis, pugilemve equamve
  Dicit, et centum potiore signis
      Munere donat.

                    Hor. l. iv., o. ii.

  * The rapture with which the Theban Swan
  has been read by every one capable of feeling the
  force of poetry, drew from Horace that beautiful
  encomium —

  Monte decurrens velut amnis, imbris
  Quem super notas aluere ripas,
  Fervet, immensusque ruit profundo.

          Pindarus ore. ibid. lib. iv., o. ii.

the Olympic Games, was the first also who sang the victories of its champions.

In short, he who first had the honor of having his name enrolled at the head of the list was Corebus the cook,* a man not less learned than modest.

Nor did the lyric poets alone avail themselves of the rich and harmonious language of magirology. From their mouths it passed into those of every bard who drew from the Castalian spring. The dramatic writers also caught the general sentiment, and cooks became the favourite characters of their dramatis personarum. Their presence on the stage became so po-

---

* Athen. Deipn. lib. ix., c. xvii., p. 382.

pular, the language of their dialogue
so palatable, that no piece could produce any interest, none could give
satisfaction to the public taste, where
the cook did not make a principal
figure. These delicious entertain-
ments, stuffed with culinary dainties,
soon, and justly, acquired the appellation of *farce*.* What would Terence
have been without his Sanga;† or, how
insignificant his ragged regiment, had
it not been headed by the general of

---

* Dr. Johnson, in his Dictionary, who appears
to have had but a confined view of this word, derives it from the French *farcer* to play the fool,
whereas it ought to belong to the family of
farcio.

† No one can read Terence without feeling his
humour. But whoever wishes to see that humour
admirably represented, should go to the plays
acted by the Westminster boys. They will then

the kitchen? It would have been vapid and insignificant as a modern tragedy without murders and ghosts, spectres and monsters, dogs and horses ;* or a comedy divested of the false sentiment, and sapping principles of German morality.

The inhabitants of Latium, tired at last of Sabine life, and the frugal diet of their ancestors, resolved upon a

witness one of the most chaste and classical treats that any country can afford.

* This lamentable departure from the chaste drama cannot be too much reprobated. The horses and the dog Gellert might be very pretty at Astley's theatre; but to see such representations on the regular classical stage, one would suppose the manager to be some " *imberbis ju renis,*" who having broke loose from his tutor—
" *Gaudet equis canibusque.*"

change of system. Sicily * was at that time the cradle of culinary science, and quickly furnished them with the best instructed artists. And so rapidly did the Romans improve under their tuition, that they not only fell in love with the art itself, but even with the language that conveyed it. The Latin, consequently, fell into contempt in the kitchen, and no one ventured to speak of its concerns but in Greek.† Let us hope that the French will never experience the same fate, or that the laboratory of the kitchen, like the new nomenclature of the chymists, or the

---

* Non Siculæ dapes
    Dulcem elaborabunt saporem.—*Hor.* lib. iii.
                    † Omnia Græcè,
Cum sit turpe magis nostris nescire Latinè.
                        Juv. Sat. vi.

jargon of empiricism, will ever be Hellenized. For there is something in
the French so delightful to the ear, so
animating to the spirits, so soft, and so
expressive of every thing that conveys
an idea of consummate excellence in
culinary art, that even the beauty of
magirological Greek must yield to it
in harmony. Admiring as I do the
Greek, the Latin, and the French languages, I am still desirous that each
should preserve its due place in society. The kitchen has an exclusive
claim to the French, but there let us
keep it. " *Facit indignatio versum,*"
said the great Roman satirist,* with
more bitterness than I am willing to
express ; but I cannot conceal that
indignation first made me seize the

---

* Juvenal, Sat. i.

pen ; and I cannot contain my bile
when I hear my mother tongue dena-
tionalized—

> " Non possum ferre, quirites,
> *Francam* urbem."
>
> *Juvenal,* Sat. vi.

Is it to be endured that all our terms
of speech are to be altered, all our
English phrases metamorphosed into
a kind of dog French?* Must an army
suffer a demoralization ? Cannot our
gallant soldiers pass a bridge without
running their heads against a *tête-de-
pont ?* May they not be allowed to
sleep under the poor shelter of a few
boughs without being *bivouaced ?*
hear unconcerned the whistling of bul-

---

† Hoc sermone pavent, hoc iram, guadia, curas.
Hoc cuncta effundunt animi secreta.
> *Juv.* Sat. vi.

lets round their heads, but with *sang
froid ;* advance upon their enemy, but
by a *pas de charge ;* or pursue him,
but with *l'épée dans les reins ?* or,
lastly, fall gallantly in the field without being put *hors de combat?* In the
midst of my indignation, however, it
is some satisfaction to know that the
French can have nothing *comfortable*
without us, and that even our *disap-
pointments* have become *theirs.**.——

This consideration gives me temper
to proceed in my history. I know
how necessary it is to keep myself
cool where I am destined to move no
where but in a heated laboratory ; I
can never quit the blazing faggot but for

---

* The French language had, for a long time,
no words to convey our ideas of comfortable and
disappointment, and they were constrained at last
to borrow ours, and have them naturalized ; and
their authors now use them.

the suffocating charcoal, and where, if I
fall out of the frying-pan, it must in-
evitably be into the fire.

The Romans having once acquired
a taste for good living, soon left all
their predecessors far behind them in
alimentary science.   Never had the
culinary art more exalted masters, or
more industrious scholars! No sooner
were these epicurean masters of the
world thoroughly initiated in the delights of the palate, than heaven,
earth, and seas, were ransacked to procure them dainties.   Nothing escaped
their devouring lust : even snails and
worms were fattened for their maws.
The varieties which they contrived to
collect, together with the records of
their feasts, are so numerous and astonishing, that, notwithstanding the
pretensions of modern gastronomy,

science looks back, absolutely dismay-
ed, at the mass of culinary talent which
that æra developed. The parks, the
lepories, the aviaries, the fisheries, the
snaileries, the orchards, vineyards, gardens, apiaries, theatres; baths, and various luxuries the Romans possessed,
would require volumes to describe.
Amongst the noble gastrologists, however, none shone more conspicuous
upon the stage than the three Apicii
—men as learned in the closet as they
were expert in the field.

The treatise of Cælius Apicius, *de
Arte Coquinariá*, will ever remain a
monument of his talent. The voyage
of another to the coast of Asia in
search of a lobster to improve the breed
of his astacery,* and his noble resolution to die rather than submit to starve

---

* The Romans had salt water preserves for

out the remainder of his life on the
poor pittance of little more than a million pounds sterling, the miserable
wreck of the once enormous fortune
which he had literally *eaten up*, are
instances of enterprize and magnani-
mity, which the modern gastrophilist
cannot fail to admire. What shall we
say of the little snug feasts of Mæ-
cenas, the choice flasks of Massic and
Falernian that he and his merry friend
Horace * quaffed together ; or how

---

feeding different kinds of sea-fish : they were
called *vivaria*—

" Non dubitaturi fugitivum dicere piscem
Depastrumque diu *vivaria* Cæsaris."

The fish in the ponds of Lucullus sold for 25,000*l.*
sterling at his death.

* Sume, Mecænas, cyathos amici,
Sospitis centum, et vigiles lucernas
Prefer in lucem, procul omnis esto
Clamor et ira.
Hor. lib. iii., od. viii.

describe the "noctes cœnasque Deûm" of the Sabine Farm?

Although the Romans did not deal much with gross morsels, yet no people enjoyed more than they the supreme happiness of an insatiate appetite. But even thus enviably endowed, they were too wise to expend its strength injudiciously or unworthily. We find, therefore, that they always picked out the tit-bits of birds, the milts of fishes,* the teats of a sow † just before she was about to farrow, and when they were turgid with the new secretion of the lacteal fluid. They delighted in the tongues of singing birds, the brains of animals, the livers of geese, and the wings of pregnant

---

* Ilia Rhombi.—*Hor. Sat.*

† Mammas suminis.—*Mart. Ep.*

hares.* The tender kid and rumpless
doves † were in high estimation, and
certainly, not least, "vulvâ nil pulchrius
amplâ." The wild boar, "animal prop-
ter convivia natum," and the oncager‡
also made their appearance. These
were the " *cœnæ capita*," to which
the more craving guests, the "*latrantes
stomachi*," were constrained to have
recourse.§ But even such, like a

---

* Fæcundæ leporis sapiens sectabitur armos.
Hor. lib. ii., Sat. iv.
† —sine clune palumbes.—*Hor.* lib.
‡ The oncager, or wild ass, was much esteemed, as also their foals, which were called *lali-
siones.—Plin. Nat. Hist.* l. viii., c. xliv.

§ Upon particular occasions, a wild boar used
to be dressed whole, and stuffed with all kinds
of animals, one within another; this dish was
called the *Trojan Horse.* The Christmas pie, in
Yorkshire, is built upon the same plan. They
had also pyramids of birds, from a peacock at the

quick-sighted alderman, who picks
out of the turtle tureen the pieces of
green fat, and leaves the coarser veal
behind, generally got hold of a favourite cut.

Ye noble Romans! so proud of
your Trojan descent, that nothing
would go down with your august Emperor but that the blood of Venus and
Æneas flowed in his veins, how vast
were all your plans! how exquisitely
refined were all your ways! With

---

base to the most diminutive wren at the summit.
The passion for *engastration* seems to have had
its admirers in all ages. The Irish Protestants,
when they met annually to celebrate King William's memory, used to construct their curse on
the Stewarts upon the same principle.—" May
the Pretender be in the Pope's belly, the Pope
in the Devil's, the Devil in Hell, and the keys
in an Orange-man's pocket."

what care you nurtured, and with what religious zeal you daily sacrificed the most costly victims on the altars of the *Père de Famille*,* a deity most piously worshipped in your age, and not less reverently adored in ours!

The Romans might be said to make three or four meals a day, although Cicero (whom we can only regard as a milksop) asserted that no man ought to make more than two. The morning was generally ushered in with oysters, eggs, and other light ware; not but some of the first-rate *Helluones* contrived to have more solid furniture. Then came the *prandium*, which seemed to correspond with the modern luncheon, or early dinner.

---

* An expression for the stomach.

Macr. Saturn, lib. vii., c. iv,

But their principal force was reserved for the evening *cæna*, or τὸ ἄριστον of the Greeks. This serious business generally began about sun-set,* and when some choice souls, some of the "*dulces animæ*," met, they kept up the " feast of reason," pretty late;† or, if the party was of a more intemperate description, they called for the "*majores calices*," and only reeled home with the morning sun,‡ which led that arch wag Martial to observe,

" Hesterno fœtare mero qui credit Acerram
" Fallitur, ad lucem semper Acerra bibit."

---

* Supremo te sole domi, Torquate, manebo.
Hor. Epist.

† ———————licebit
Æstivam sermoni benigno tendere noctem.
Hor.

‡ Sic noctem pateiâ sic ducem carmine, donec
Injiciat radios in mea vina dies.
Prop. 1. iv., E. vi.

The table was usually decorated with flowers.* They were served with three courses ; and the guests reclined on couches.† The *first* course generally opened the campaign, by affording some slight skirmishing with oysters, cockles, eggs, cheese, and vegetables, just to whet their appetites. The *second* soon followed. Then there was no longer child's play : " fervet opus :" fish, flesh, fowl, in endless succession, crowded upon the board, till human powers could do no more. A saving moment for breathing ensued, till the *third* arrived. This in-

---

* ———potare, et sparsere flores
Incipiam.—*Hor. Epist.*

† Si potes Achaiis conviva recumbere lectis.
                              Hor. Epist.
Languidus in cubitum jam se conviya reponet.—*Hor.* lib. ii., Sat. iv.

troduced fruits, fresh and preserved,
nuts, cakes and wines, like our des-
serts ; religious libations to the gods
followed, and the worshippers of Bacchus never retired till they had a *skin-
full.**

With the decline of the Roman empire, the arts perished, science decayed, gastrology lost its patrons, and
the kitchen received a rude shock.
We are under the necessity, therefore,
of passing by these ages of ignorance :
we must omit noticing the barba-
rism of the Franks ; and suspend upon
their racks the *spits*, which so
unmercifully overthrew the *seeth-
ing* pots of the Gauls. We will set

---

* Whether this term arose from the skins
which held the wine, or the persuasion that the
skin of the religious worshipper of Bacchus
could hold no more without bursting, I leave for
the learned to decide.

aside the roast-worship * of Charlemagne and his academy, where never
a word of good French was spoken.†

---

* It appears by the Chronicles of St. Denis
(liv. 3) that Charlemagne had a great liking for a
good roast, but none for a physician; of which
the following extract will shew :—" Aussi comme
contre cœur (because he did not like physicians)
pour ce que ils li faisoient mengier char cuite en
yarc (that is boiled) et li defendoient les roz
(roasted) que il mengoit volontiers comme il avoit
toujours accoustume ; and a little after is added ;
" Accoustumement estoit chacun jour de quatre
pair de mis (eight entries) tant seulment sans li
roz dont li vencour (huntsmen) li servoient et de
celui mengoit il plus volontiers qui di nul autre.

† During the era of Charlemagne, they spoke
in France what was called la langue *Tyoise*,
which was derived from *Teuton*, the name of the
ancient Germans, and from whence comes Teu-
tonic : but the language of the third epoch having combined with it many Latin words, was
called Romans, or Romance.

Smiling at the conceits of the Knights
of the round Table, and their partialities
for whales, seals, porpoises, cranes,* and

---

* The passion for all kinds of birds was very
prevalent in this age, and particularly for cranes;
birds which the Romans had held in estimation—
" Discerpta ferentes
Magna gruis, sparsi sale multo." *Hor. Sat.*
The English bills of fare formerly abounded with
them also, and the Italians also considered them excellent meat, as the following little anecdote will
shew :—

A rich nobleman in Florence held in great
estimation the crane, a bird which is now lightly
regarded. Wishing to entertain some friends, he
shot one, and immediately sent it to his cook,
whose name was Doribas, with orders to roast it.
Whilst the crane was on the spit, a servant girl,
a very intimate *friend* of Doribas's, and rather
rounder than a vestal, came into the kitchen;
and, attracted by the odour of the roasting bird,
insisted upon having a leg of it. Doribas re-
fused, Gonette, (for that was her name) became

bitterns ; and passing by those unproductive ages when mankind knew as

---

more importunate; and at last the poor cook,
not ignorant of her condition, gave up the point.
His embarrassment became great, and he was
quite at a loss how to serve up the mutilated bird
at his master's table.   He at last turned it down
upon that side where the leg was wanting : the
deficiency was soon discovered—the lord grew
very angry, and ordered his cook immediately
into his presence.   The poor man, quite at a loss
for an excuse, boldly asserted that cranes never
had more than one leg, and that he had seen a
thousand such.   His master, quite outrageous at
this piece of impudence, was on the point of
caning and dismissing him on the spot, when his
friends interfered, and argued that it was pos-
sible the man might have seen cranes of this description ; and that, to decide the matter, it
would be advisable to have a chase the next day.
To this Doribas was obliged to consent, and went
out quite in despair at his forlorn state.   The
party were not long before they found a flock of

little respecting the elegant use of a
tongue as the elegant dressing of one,
we will pause for a moment to contemplate St. Louis.* This monarch
was the true restorer of the House of

---

cranes—Doribas first discovered them quietly re-
posing, as is their custom, upon one leg. The
happy cook exultingly called out—" See, gentlemen, see if what I advanced be not true ; they
have but *one leg*." " Pob !" cried his lord,
" you shall see in a minute that they have *two*."
he shouted, " Ohe ! ohe ! wheu ! wheu !" —The
cranes flew off and distinctly shewed two long
legs behind them."—" Pest !" cried the cook,
" if I had known the secret when I served the
crane on the table, I would have shouted, ohe !
ohe ! wheu ! wheu ! too, and then my crane
might have found his other leg also." The company laughed heartily, and the cook was pardoned.

* Louis 9, called St. Louis, mounted the throne
in 1226.

Sorbonne, and the original founder of
that magirological learning which has
since contributed so much to the honor and glory of France, and to the
edification and happiness of her neighbours.

This prince, so unfortunate in his
campaigns beyond sea, made full repa-
ration to his country for every disaster
he brought upon it, by the initiation
of a variety of artists in all the culinary secrets of the East. Though he
was unable to rescue the Cross from
the hands of infidels, still the sound
of trumpet and beat of drum, taken
from the Saracens, announced with
triumph his return. Too much exul-
tation could not be expressed, nor too
much gratitude shewn, for the spices
that he brought from Asia; and in
comparison of which, the price of his

campaigns, the blood that had been spilt, and the treasures that had been expended, were of little moment. Every belle, and every beau, the most renowned knight, or the most rigid monk, welcomed alike the cinnamon, the nutmeg, the ginger, the pepper, and the clove: the chroniclers, romancers, and poets; historians, actors, and troubadours, joined with one accord to celebrate their praises, as the most exquisite adjuncts to the table, and yielding the most delightful sensations to the palate. The nutmeg, in particular, has ever been received with singular distinction, so that a French poet said of it—

" Aimez vous la Muscade, on en a mit partout."
Boil. Sat.

E

The spices * came very fortunately to the aid of the crusaders, who, in the course of their sea voyages had had frequently to contend with morsels that had set all the artillery of their jaws † at defiance. But it is surprizing to find their posterity, without being reduced to the same extremities or hardships, should preserve their bill of fare ; and, as if out of respect to their memory, continue it even to the reign of John the Second,

---

* All the manuscripts which remain of this period abound in praise of the spices. The old poets compare them to the most fragrant perfumes. The facility of our intercourse with the East now has occasioned them to be treated with less veneration, although their loss would create a piercing outcry.

† L'Artillerie de Gucule, an expression of Rabelais.

called the Good.* Surely it is not necessary, because at sea we are constrained to make acquaintance with
sea-hogs and sea-dogs, that there is
the smallest obligation to keep up the
connection on shore.†

In the reign of Charles the Fifth,‡
says Le Sage, they began to be a little
more refined in their tastes, and to become acquainted with some excellent
condiments. Whilst this prince was lay-

---

* John II., called le Bon, of the house of Va-
lois, mounted the throne of France in 1350—
v. Fawkes's Chronology.

† We find that seals and porpoises constituted
a part of the bill of fare, even in the famous banquet given at the enthonement of Neville, Arch-
bishop of York, in 1434. At present they are
only retained in that of Kamchatsca.

‡ Charles V., called " le sage et riche," succeeded to the throne in 1364.

ing the *foundation* of his famous library of the kings of France, Taillevant, the chief officer of his kitchen, was sapping the *foundations* of the boiling system amongst his subjects.

As when a brisk gale precedes the approach of morn, and drives away the clouds which obscure the sky, ushering in Aurora in all her radiant smiles, and cheering us with the rays of the rising sun—so, Taillevant, the genial zephyr and harbinger of an heavenly day, shot forth, and throwing aside the veil which concealed from us the brilliant fires of an enlightened age, dazzled us with their unusual splendour. Like another Prometheus, he seemed to have stolen some of the sparks of heaven to illumine his stoves, and kindle the fires of his culinary laboratory, where this exalted genius,

solely occupied with the objects of
science, or in exercising the charitable
disposition of feeding the hungry, soon
brought his art to the summit of perfection. He chopped, minced, harden-
ed, softened, liquified, baked, roasted,
broiled, stewed, fricaseed, braized,
glazed, and new modelled, at his pleasure, every thing that came under the
power of his fashioning hand, and
then introduced them in all the parade
of new and sumptuous apparel to the
table of his master.* There they appeared in such variety of shapes ; so
altered and so bedizened ; so decked

---

* This patriarch of the kitchen taught his
pupils the method of roasting eggs and butter
upon the spit, and other secrets now lost, or of
such difficult execution, that modern artists
shrink from the attempt.

out with gorgeous accompaniments; some swimming in *sauce blanche*, some in *noire*, some in *sauce piquante*, *Robert*, *à l'Alose*, *à la compotte*, *à la moutarde*, *à l'ail*, *à la créme*, *chaude*, *froide*, *rouge*, *vèrte*, *jaune*, &c. that they were exhibited in perfect masquerade. Even vegetables were so metamorphosed, that their characters were totally altered : they appeared to have assumed a new feature ; and, like the grafted tree of Virgil, each wondered at the change and novelty of its own figure.

" Miraturque novas frondes, et non sua poma."

In order to shew his gratitude for these benefits, Charles bestowed a splendid livery upon all the officers of his kitchen. Indeed, he pushed his taste so far on this occasion, that all the ministers of his household, and even the magistrates of Paris, were ordered to dress themselves like *des Poulets au Bedeau,** that is to say, in party-coloured robes.

Taillevant in his turn, again, sensible of his royal master's condescension, prepared his *Vivandier*† for its reception into the library of the Louvre; and, notwithstanding the care with which the press has multiplied works of this nature, it has been

---

* To the English admirer of a plain roasted barn-door fowl, it may, perhaps, excite some astonishment to hear that a *poulet au bedeau* assumes a very different appearance, and is exhibited in two distinct colours. Indeed, at all the dinners of a top-rate French cook, the inexperienced will do well to have in mind " nimium ne crede colori."

† Vivandier, the title of Taillevant's work.

so greedily devoured, that if the book had appeared in these days, I verily believe the sheets themselves would have been swallowed up for the delicacies they contain.

The flight of Taillevant was too elevated. He soared with such eagle wings—he took such giant strides in his magirological career, that his rivals were quite in despair, and none would venture to advance beyond the bounds which he had proscribed : all humbly followed his steps, as children who play at "*follow the leader*."

Some time after this period, a stranger, who was by no means of the *same kidney*, dared to shew himself upon the stage with Taillevant. This was an Italian of the name of Platina : a man the best instructed of his age in all the learning of the Vatican. He appeared to be completely *larded* and *stuffed* with Greek and Latin. The fear of wounding the delicate ears of the sovereign pontiff, and those of Cardinal Rovella, (that kind and *clement** patron under whose auspices he had made his début,) engaged him to alter the title of his work, so as to do away all idea that it contained any thing too luscious. He consequently gave it the appellation of the " Honest Voluptuary."† Under this seducing form it was quickly translated from

---

* The Cardinal Rovella took the title of St. *Clement* when he became cardinal.

† Platina dedicated his work to the cardinal under the title " *Platina de honestâ Voluptate et Valetudine.*"—The French translation, *L'honeste Volupte*, by Christol, has often been printed at Lyons, as may be seen in the gastrological library.

the Italian into French ; and although
the most fastidious critics allowed the
production the merit of being perfectly chaste, yet they could not help
finding fault, that it was more sweet
than voluptuous.

The *patine* of this Italian, filled
with nothing but chickens' heads and
fennels, appeared so contemptible by
the side of the French dishes, loaded
with majestic heads of calves and
heads of brocoli, that to have opposed
one to the other, would have been
something like setting an Italian grey-
hound to fight an English bull-dog.

Platina seized a very unfavourable
moment to push himself into notice.
It was at the very period when the
gentlemen of the hardware trade
had succeeded in giving a mortal blow
throughout France to the old dynasty

of earthern pots, and consolidated the reign of brass and copper, by depriving their adversaries of the whistle.* Notwithstanding the judgment against Platina was very general, he was not without merit, and his dishes got the name of *Patina Catelonica*, or Catalonian dish. His advocates were loud in his praise, and honoured Spain for having given him birth. The same country also nurtured in her bosom *Roberto da Nola*, a magirological artist of the most transcendent genius. His great rival, *Martino Martinez*, did not appear till the following age. Every amateur will regret that these

---

* It may be necessary to notice that these foreign braziers, in order to save their voices, used a whistle instead of crying their trade about the streets.

great artists trained up no pupils in
their opsartytical schools, and that the
bad taste and apathy of the Spaniards
made them abandon the solid literature of the table for the empty record
of feasts.

The Portuguese also, the original
conquerors of the spice countries, satisfied with the laurels they had acquired, seemed to partake of the apathy of their neighbours. Nor was
any attempt made to rouse them from
this inglorious languor, till, in the
present age, Don Lucas Rigaud published his culinary art, *(Nova Arte de
Cozingha,)* a work of some merit.

Let those independent spirits who,
under the protection of the triumphant
flag of Great Britain, sought the shores
of Brasil, return again to their native
stoves. They may now repose in per-

fect safety. Lusitania demands their presence. The victorious arms of the great Wellington have left them nothing further to dread from those legions of devouring ultra-montane locusts that overran their country ; drained their soup kettles to their very dregs, and ravaged every thing before them. What a brilliant moment now presents itself! what a glorious opportunity to give immortality to their retreat, and come home laden with the delicious nutriments of that vast and productive * continent, which opened its arms to receive them !

---

* Whoever wishes to form an idea of the exquisite productions of the Brasils, may consult the natural history of that country inserted in the History of the Revolutions of Portugal, by L'Abbé Vertot, with a continuation and description of Brasil, by *Louis de Boisgelin, Knight of Malta.*

The Italians displayed a very different taste from either the Spaniards or the Portuguese. During two centuries (as would be easy to convince any one in this enlightened age of gastronomy) the theatre of Italy displayed before an admiring people, artists of a very superior cast. Amongst these were officers of health, and doctors of physic. Such was *Michel Savanarola*, decorated with the Cross of Malta: such was *Pesanelli*, *Peravisino*, and *Gallina*.—Men who instructed their patients to play with admirable address on the alimentary stage, whether they had to exhibit on days of fast or days of feast—although some severe critics accused them of *mouthing their parts*. Many of the under-strappers also were admirable professors of magirology : such were *Roselli*, *Maestro*, *Geovanne*, *Messi-*

bargo, Scappi, Il Valente, Pandini,
Robasso, Magnani, Cervio, and *Ste-*
fani, who taught the best method of
garnishing and ornamenting dishes.—
These students of culinary arts, had
all passed their examinations, and
received the graduate honors of gastronomy. Amongst which we find
Rosetti, il Cavaliero, Reale, Fusorito,
Lancelotti, Colorosi, Liberati, Mattci,
and many others who have given spe-
cimens of their talents, worthy the attention of every amateur. But it is a
matter of surprize to find that Geovanne, archmagirist of the Vatican ;
Scappi, secret cook of Pope Pius
V., and Romoli, surnamed *Pononto,*
produced works in Italy in the 16th
century, which *Massialot, Marin,*
Menon, Le Cointre, or even *Viard*
himself, would not have been ashamed

to own, either for elegance of composition, or solidity of matter.

The description which Scappi has left us of his kitchen artillery at the holding of a conclave, is a chef-d'œuvre of taste and ingenuity in this species of *armoury*. I would here give it in detail, only I should fear that if it were in the presence, and invited a comparison with the cradle spits and hook spits, with the roasters and digesters, the stew pans, the sauce pans, and the fry pans, of the present day, that it would be considered of no more consequence than one of Manton's pistols by the side of *Queen Anne's pocket-piece.** But that the

* The name of a large piece of ordnance in the tower, respecting which the Ciceroni never fails (if there be no ladies present) to entertain his company with a little traditionary wit.

reader may not be entirely in the dark
on this interesting topic and unin-
formed respecting this fulminating
battery of the conclave, or the account
which Scappi has left us, I will observe that it must have required a legion of engineers to have worked it;
and a demi-brigade, at least, of the
most robust braziers to have kept his
park of artillery in serviceable condition.

There appears to be no doubt, but
as far back as the 14th century, that
the princes of Italy drew their arch-
magirists from the schools of France ;
and that, moreover, they even sent
their own youth, whom they destined
for the profession, to receive their education at Paris. No one can question
the authority of an Italian fanatic* who

---

* Pogge, a Florentine, born at Rome in 1380.

speaks out upon this point in plain
terms.—" A Duke of Milan," says he,
" had a very excellent cook, whose
studies had been completed at Paris.
For a long time the prince was perfectly
satisfied with the state of his kitchen.
One day, however, he sent for him, and,
with much anger declared, that the
dinners which he had lately served,
were detestable—' Monseigneur,' an-
swered the cook, ' my dinners would
have been equally excellent as formerly, if, unluckily, it had not been for
some troublesome fellows who spoiled
my sauces :'—' Hey ! what is that
you say ?' exclaimed the Duke ;
' who has had the audacity to come

This extract is taken from his " Amusing Anec-
dotes." And is to be found in " Les Mélanges
tirés d'une grande Bibliothèque (tom 20, p. 87).

into my kitchens ?'—' Monseigneur,'
replied the cook, ' pardon me—no
one comes into your kitchens, nor
even near them : the people to whom
I allude, are these d——d Florentines
with whom you are at war, and whose
success has taken away, your appetite—gain but a victory over them,
and depend upon it that you will find
my dishes as good as ever.' "—In
this anecdote it is not only gratifying
to find that cooks can shew flashes of
wit, like the flashes of their labora-
tories ; but it is an additional pleasure
to find great humour and transcendent
professional genius united in the same
person.

Let no one say that the spirit of
gastrophilism never found its way
within the walls of the Vatican, unless
he would see, rising up as it were from

their graves, myriads of monks, pre-
lates, and sovereign pontiffs, to give
the lie to such an assertion—and
above all would stand forth the ve-
nerable shades of Paul II. and Clement VII.* who died heroically in
the bed of honour, not in defending
the Tarpeian *rock* against its invaders,
but in a desperate affair wherein he
was engaged with *a Rock Cantaleupe.*
Nor let any one maintain, that the
god of wine was not worshipped, and
had no altar erected to him within the

* Clement VII was supposed to owe his death
to the indigestion of a melon. It was during his
pontificate that Rome was sacked by Bourbon,
and soon after which it was said 8000 young
women were found to be pregnant; a circumstance which gave rise to insinuations that no
great resistance had been made to their robust
ravishers.

private chambers of the popes, unless
he would see Benedict XII. throw
aside the veil, and display the libations which he made amidst the circle
of his numerous courtiers—libations
so abundant, that they gave rise to the
proverb—" to drink like a pope *"—
Culinary artists were no where more
considered than in Italy, and particularly by the sons of the church. We
are told, amongst other cardinals, that
Hypolitus, belonging to the Medici
family, gave a thousand ducats a year
to a Portuguese archmagirist and carving esquire, together with an appointment of a carriage and horses, and the

* One reads in Balure's lives of the popes,
that Benedict XII. was, " Potator vini maximus
ab omnibus curialibus dicebatur, adeò ut versum
sit in proverbium consuetum dici, *bibamus pa-
paliter.*

promise ef a pension of 150 or 200 louis d'ors, whenever the fatigues of service should make it necessary for him to retire. Nor were they held in less esteem by the laity, who, if they had not the means of paying them so handsomely as the clergy, made up for it by the most respectful and humble deportment, never venturing to address them but by the title of *Magnifico Signor.* Alexander Vacchi, a citizen of Venice, (a town where titles are not bestowed with too much facility,) wrote to a simple cook of Venice, one of his intimate acquaintance, whom he addressed—

Al magnifico Signor Padron mio osservandissimo il Signor Matteo Barbini Cuoco, et Scalio celeberrimo della Citta di Venetia.

Amongst the gastrological authors

of Italy at that period, we must not
omit Massonio, who wrote a *little
work*, not containing more than an
hundred sheets, solely upon the manner of dressing a salad. About an
hundred years after him our countryman Evelyn resumed this subject—a
work not so voluminous as the former, and one which would have been
excellent, had he but added a thun-
dering philippic against those despotic
squires who oblige their guests to stir
up their own salad ;* an inconve-

---

* There is no question in gastronomy that has
produced so much controversy as the mode of
dressing a salad. A transcendent genius, whose
name is, I fear, lost to science, appeared some
years back on the alimentary theatre of London,
and undertook to settle all difficulties by dressing salads at half-a-guinea each ! !

nience which not only occasions considerable delay to the eager gastrophilist, but at the same time gives a crude
taste to the lettuce. In England,
which has the character (as Mr.
Cobbett never fails to tell his readers
weekly) of being a *thinking nation*,
where the people are strongly attach-
ed to their habits of life, and extreme-
ly jealous of innovation, they delayed
much longer than in Italy, and in
France, before they gave any attention
to the delicacies of the table. Nor,
perhaps, did the art lose much by their
forbearance. A bill of fare, however,
has been preserved, of a banquet* given

---

* Leland relates that sixty-two cooks were employed to dress this feast, and gives an account
of all the dishes, and manner in which they were
served.

at the enthronement of Neville, Arch-
bishop of York, in the 14th century,
which does as great honour to the
genius of his grace's archmagirist, as
it does to the appetites of his guests.
Thanks! immortal thanks! to the
society of antiquarians who rescued
from the dust of the library, " Receipts on Ancient Cookery," curious
monuments of alimentary science in
the 14th, 15th, and 16th centuries.
The monks, however, of the 14th century, were not so much behind hand
as the laity in the great business of
eating. The chief cook of a monastery
was a personage of the first rate dignity; and that brother was always
elected to the office who had shewn
most industry and pious zeal in the
attainment of gastrological excellence.
The historian of Croyland Abbey tells

F

us that Chateris, cook of that establishment, moved by the love of God and
the interests of religion, gave forty
pounds (no mean sum in those days)
that the convent might have orgeat on
fish days to drink with their bread and
honey. Nor were the secular clergy,
if not equally refined, by any means
backward in promoting the good cause
of eating and drinking to the utmost
of their power. They· had even the
ingenuity to make their religious ceremonies aid their gluttony. These re-
verend theogastrophilists established,
therefore, masses five times a year,
where, in praise of the holy Virgin,
they met to commit the most beastly
debauches. Their churches became
taverns and brothels.—Clergy and
laity, rolling over each other, exhibited scenes corresponding more with

Bacchic orgies, than any thing con-
nected with Christian worship. These
revels justly acquired the name of
glutton masses.

From the commencement of about
the year sixteen hundred, we find the
English gastrologists beginning to push
their acquaintance with foreign artists,
and to translate their works into their
own language. The most ancient
that has come to my knowledge, is the
Italian banquet of the Sieur Roselli,
one which would now be held in no
great estimation.

In Germany, where the people reason deeply upon all subjects that come
before them, and where more of the
primitive powers of appetite seem to
prevail than in other countries, the
demands of the *paunch* have always
been considered of the first import-

ance. The table of the German consequently continues to offer for our
observation the most enormous joints;
where, if fortunately you have a
stomach bomb proof, and escape ex-
plosion on the field, you must sicken
out the night under a distressing load
of molten grease.

When the culinary art of Apicius
first found its way to the press of Germany, they added to the *Kuchenmeis-
terey*,* a little work of the same de-
description. Thus the alimentary
theatre in the country of the *Cimbri*
and the *Teutons*, always filled with
great actors, has never failed to exhibit
compositors who could both write

---

* There is an edition of this work very well
preserved in the library of the Royal Society at
London; Küchenmeisterey, or Culinary Arts.

and perform ;—no less artists in theory, than mechanics in practice. There was a publication, however, in Latin, by *Vellichius*, which, considering the time it appeared, is much to be esteemed ; and another written in Italian by Giegher Bavarais, carving esquire to the German nation at Padua. This rare work not only teaches us some very pretty delicacies, but also the proper method of cutting them up : it besides tells us what is very important to know, that the young Germans who frequented the university, liked to attend to the body as well as the mind.

Harsz-dorffern, or *Hartdorffern*, which sweet and harmonious name, in whatever manner it may be written, or pronounced, and bearing evident marks of the country which bestowed it. This Hartdorffern, I was going to observe, translated the work of his countryman Giegher into German, with some additions which will ensure its preservation in the memory of even ingratitude itself.

In Holland, in Denmark, Sweden,* and Poland, where the people are generally notorious theogastrophilists, and enjoying vast capabilities of appetite,

---

* It is in vain that Linnæus has instructed his countrymen, the Swedes, in all the nutritive productions of the two worlds. It is in vain that he has attempted to teach, in his *Culina Mutata,* why the chymical kitchen has excluded from its laboratory certain aliments which would have done honour to the Apician stoves. Notwithstanding all he has said and done, the greatest part of Sweden is still plunged in the darkness of Scandinavian gastroworship—" Quæque ipse miserrima vidi."

they have but few magirologists. The
alimentary works of the Germans are,
with few exceptions, the only publications to be found amongst them.
And they continue to besmear with
currant-jelly their haunch of venison,
roasted to a rag, and generally stink-
ing abominably into the bargain—hor-
resco referens.

We will now return to France, and
take up our history at the period
where Taillevant, the great patriarch
of the kitchen, closed his mortal career. Not to eulogise such a man
would be unpardonable. That the
gratitude of posterity may not be with-
held, they should know that they owe
to his clear and enlightened mind the
principal happiness that they *now
taste.* He lived under three monarchs
He never once quitted the service of

his legitimate sovereigns. His talents were the constant theme of their praise ; and he might be said literally to die in his *master s mouth.*

The troubles which agitated France during the reigns of Charles VI. and Charles VII., almost proved fatal to that infant kitchen to which Taille-vant had given birth. The Dukes of Burgundy lent it all the aid in their power, and that part which they trans-planted into their own domains cer-tainly flourished beyond all expecta-tion and Olivia de la Marche has fur-nished us with some descriptions of the Flemish and Burgundian banquets of this period, worthy the notice of the most difficult amateur.

The cruel Louis the Eleventh, so lean in person, that he went by the name of the walking anatomy, drew to

his court a swarm of priests for the direction of his conscience, and the sal-
vation of his soul, and amused himself
by paying in the most absurd and pro-
fuse manner the officers of health who
had the care of his body. This was a
disposition by no means calculated to
recal the emigrants of the kitchen to
the bosom of their country, or to en-
courage any foreign artist of merit to
settle under his patronage.

The death, however, of this monarch,
accompanied by a political event
somewhat singular, fortunately restored good living to France, when it
seemed at its very lowest ebb. The
taking of Constantinople* by a nation

---

* Constantinople was taken by the Turks under Mahomet II., in 1452. It was an event that
occasioned a great sensation in the Christian

who lighted the fires which were to heat their baths with the learning of libraries, who never permitted the juice of the grape to touch their lips, and who recoiled at the very sight of a pig, caused all the Grecian artists to spread themselves over Italy. Their arrival in that country produced a complete revolution in the gastronomical horizon, and of which the 'French, at all times lovers of novelty, were desirous to take a nearer view.

This new crusade, without being

---

world. All were called upon in defence of the Cross. Amongst others, we are told that the Duke of Burgundy swore upon the body of a roasted pheasant, and called upon his courtiers to join him, that he would march an army to dislodge the Turks. They *performed* upon the pheasant with great avidity; but he certainly never *performed* his oath.

preached up by popes and bishops had shortly plenty of followers, and the King of France soon found himself at the head of a brilliant army. Unfortunately, Charles VIII., and his companions at arms, who expected in their expedition into Italy to *have caught the bird upon her nest*, were cruelly disappointed, and brought nothing back from their conquests but a few *melons** and *bons Chrétiens*, together with a certain *hot †sauce* of

---

* Melons were not known in France, says the author, *des mélanges tirés d'une grande Bibliotheque* (tom. 3. p. 13.) till Charles VIII. brought them from Italy. The pears known by the name of bons-chrétiens were introduced about the same time.

† The disease alluded to was supposed originally to be brought into Spain by the companions of Columbus. From Spain it quickly travelled to Naples, from thence into France

a most unsocial and irreligious nature,
which they acquired at Naples, and
which left the most bitter remem-
brances of its corrosive qualities,
amongst those who had been infected
with its poison.

Louis XII., who got the appellation of *le Pere du Peuple*, made
himself ridiculous by his rigid economy, both amongst his own subjects,
and those of the kitchen ; and died

(where it was called the Neapolitan disease,) and
from France into England, (where it had the appellation of the French disease.) Europe, however, in return, inflicted a still greater scourge
upon America, inasmuch as the innocent and the
guilty were alike the victims of its virulence.
The small-pox was never known on the transat-
lantic continent before the European conquest.
Thanks to the immortal Jenner; a million of lives
are now annually saved by vaccination in New
Spain !

miserably ; not because the sister of
that fat monster, Henry VIII., whom
he had married, whetted his appetite
too much ; but because she had insisted upon changing his hour of
dining.*

His successor, Francis I, the father
and restorer of letters in his dominions,
was likewise the father and restorer of
the kitchen. His misfortunes in
Italy, like those of St. Louis in Asia,

---

* " The good King Louis XII.," says a French
writer, " for the sake of his wife totally altered his
manner of living. Whereas he formerly dined at
eight o'clock in the morning, he now did not dine
till noon. He had been accustomed to go to bed
at six in the evening, and he now sat up till mid-
night." (Hist. de Chev. Bayard.) Louis was in
his 54th year when he forgot, in the arms of his
young wife, his habits of frugality and temperance, and paid the forfeit of his life in three
months after his marriage.

produced the greatest benefits to gastrology.

This monarch, by his expedition to
Pavia, where he lost every thing but
his honour* and his appetite, drew
at the same time some advantage from
his residence in Italy, where alimentary science and the other arts had
been encouraged and remunerated by
the Medici family. Leo X. and his
successors on the papal throne made
considerable progress in culinary refinement : and it happened that Francis,
having once tasted a calf at the table
of the pontif which had been fatted
upon milk, would never after eat of
any other kind of veal. The Nor-

---

* Francis, after the unfortunate battle of Pavia,
wrote to his mother the following short but expressive letter : —

" All is lost but honour."

mans, therefore, in conformity to his
taste, reared their calves entirely upon
milk, till they were six, nine, and
even twelve months old. By these
means they made those in the neigh-
bourhood of Paris and Pontoise full as
pontifical and *ecclesiastical* as those
in the environs of Rome and Sarento.
After the example of the Normans,
the Flemands, under the auspices of
Cardinal Louis de Bourbon, fattened
sheep also to the admiration of all
those who had the honor of being invited to the table of this illustrious
gastrophilist of the red hat.

Of all the exquisite fruits that Italy
offered to the notice of Francis, the
orange was the only one from which
he abstained, and this under a suspicion that Charles VIII. owed his

death to one.   Every time, therefore,
that this fruit was presented to him,
he put it back, saying he disliked its
smell. The Chancellor Du Prat, who
unquestionably liked eating as well as
his master, but with less delicacy of
taste, shewed at this time a great partiality for the young offspring of those
patiently *laboring*, and too often *be-
labored* gentry with long ears.   As,
at the brilliant epoch of Roman literature and Roman culinary science, the
first minister of Augustus regaled
upon the flesh of asses : so also the
minister of Francis I., at the celebrated period which restored the
French language to its purity, and the
French kitchen to its excellence, displayed the same taste !!   In one respect, however, there was an essen-

tial difference. Mecænas made not
only his *led captains** regale upon the
young Mid*as's* of the plains, but likewise introduced them amongst the
grandees of Rome ;† whereas Du Prat
could not persuade the most obse-
quious of his parasites, nor even the
lowest clerk in his office, to touch a
dish, however admirably dressed, where
any suspicion might arise that it contained but the tip of that animal's ear,
the abundance of which is so much
the object of admiration.

---

* Led Captains is a term applied to a description of gentry which most great men have about
them—hangers-on.   The Romans called them
" umbræ."   Quos Mecænas abduxerat umbras.

Hor. l. ii. l. 8.

† Pliny, however, tells us, that after the de-
mise of this great descendant of the Etrurian
kings, the Romans had not sufficient regard for
his memory to continue the fare.

Compege, a cotemporary author, has inserted in his Album the physicians of Francis I.: and we ought to regard the man who has preserved for posterity these precious details of the King of France and his Chancellor, as one of the most profound gastrologians who has appeared in modern history. In comparison with him, the ancient Pliny was a mere child in the science of gastronomy, and Athenæus is totally eclipsed by him. This great genius dedicated his work, and all the good things in it, to the immortal Chancellor *de l'Hopital*, as a man, the capacity of whose stomach was not less known to him, than the erudition of his palate.*

* Epist: ad Mich: Hosp. Gall: Cancell: ubi dicit, " novi enim stomachum ac palatum tuum eruditum."

Pidoux, a very ancient magirological artist, flourished also at this
period, and together with the incom-
parable author just mentioned, must
be considered as the brightest gem in
the crown of Francis. Nor let any one
suppose that because his soups got
the appellation of broths, that on that
account they bore any similitude to
those of the Lacedemonians, any more
than the modern game of goose* does

---

* The antiquity of this game is engraved upon
all the boards that are used for playing, where it
is called " revived from the Greeks." It derives
its modern name of goose in consideration of the
great estimation in which those birds were formerly held. The citizens used to club together
in *picnic* fashion to regale upon them, and the
person who won at the game had his share of the
dinner scot free. It is a game of which children
are very fond, as it requires little address, and
affords much amusement

to the ancient one, because it is called revived.

A king who conversed familiarly with his subjects at table, who was surrounded by the best informed men of the age, and who besides had very enlarged views and extensive plans, could not fail to be enlightened on whatever might contribute most to the benefit of his people. He judged it, therefore, essential to treat with all due distinction, and cherish by every kind regard, the foster-mother of Jupiter* in every part of his kingdom;

---

* The difficulties and dangers which the king of the gods experienced in his infancy are well known. Saturn, who, like a great buck rabbit, had a passion for devouring all his offspring, would have ate up the young Jupiter also, had he not been concealed from his search, where he was suckled by a sow, and fed by bees.

and foster-mother also of more than three-fourths of his subjects.* He made on her behalf the counsellors of the king, examiners of hog's tongues, with orders also to search most minutely the tongues of every one that was the least suspected. But nothing impure ever found its way from the mouth of this ancient family; which for so many ages occupied, without impediment, and without competition, the first places of the noble house of Adephagia.† Since the time of St. Louis, no monarch had

---

* There is no animal so prolific as the sow, and in many countries they are the greatest security against famine. Francis was, therefore, not wanting in penetration when he encouraged the breed.

† Adephagia was worshipped at a temple in Sicily, where swine were sacrificed on her altars.

had a kitchen so well appointed, or so well paid, as Francis I. None had given the same attention to their establishment, or had entertained in so choice a manner. Even to this day posterity has not ceased to talk with rapture of the feasts which he made for Charles V., (who, by the bye, had not entertained him with the best fare,) as well as those with which he regaled Henry VIII.,* the greatest and the fattest glutton of his age. We

---

* Henry VIII. was as fond of drinking as eating. For it is reported that in the 16th century, the wine d'Ay was so much esteemed, that the Emperor Charles V., the Pope Leo X., Francis I., and Henry VIII.; each purchased and cultivated a piece of land at Ay, where they kept their distinct vignerons, and made their own wines. Melanges tirées d'une grande—Bibl. Tom. 3. p. 66.

still delight to survey the field of
Ardres, called the field *du drap d'or*,
on account of its magnificence; where,
in company with the King of England,
he *cracked many a bottle* of excellent
wine : and we cannot but applaud the
address with which he *tripped up the
heels* of his brother monarch, unquestionably the best wrestler and the
best *two bottle man* of his kingdom.*

---

* Fleuranges relates, that the two friendly
monarchs, after witnessing the trials of strength
and skill between the English and French wrest-
lers, retired to a tent where they drank freely.
The King of England then seized the King of
France by the collar, exclaiming " Brother, I
must wrestle with you," and attempted to trip
up his heels, but the King of France, being very
expert, twisted him round and laid him on his
back.   Henry would have renewed the contest,
but was prevented.

From the period of Francis I., one may affirm that the throne of France was always filled with kings renowned for their attachment to *those little delicate morsels*, which may be considered as some counterpoise to the heavy cares which are the inseparable concomitants of a crown.

Catherine of Medicis enriched her suite with the most distinguished culinary artists, but amongst them were found some corruptors of taste who ran down the Italian kitchen. Her officers were the first who gave the Parisians a taste for the Rossolis.*

---

* It was about the year 1533 that the Italians who accompanied Catherine of Medicis into France introduced the Rossoli. Its name appears to be derived from *Ros solis*, the plant from which it is principally distilled—v. Hist. de la

The Hippocras,* proud of its antiquity, and which hitherto had never

---

vie privèe des Franc. et Mel. d'une Grande Bibl.
This liqueur (like Noyeau in Martinique) is
made good no where but in Italy.

* Soon after the introduction of the spices
into France, they found their way into wine,
together with sugar,, which came partially into
use about the same time. It was upon mixtures
of this kind that the hippocras was founded, and
was named in honour of Hippocrates, who merely added honey and cinnamon to wine. But it
owed its modern distinction to Alexis, a Pied-
montese, who made it according to the following
recipe :—Cinnamon one oz.
          Ginger two drachms.
          Cloves two penny weights.
          Nutmeg and galangal one penny weight
            of each.
These must be well pounded together, and infused in a pint of red or white wine, and another
pint of *vin de malvoisio* : a pound of the best
sugar should then be added. These are the quan-

found any liquors that had ventured
to dispute precedence with it, opposed
the most noble resistance to the pretensions of Italy; and Louis XIV.
afterwards shewed himself its zealous
defender.

Henry II., Charles IX., and Henry
III., according to the expression of a
cotemporary, had. " *leur Marmitte
tantôt haute, tantôt basse;"*—sometimes their *pot boiling*, and at other
times scarcely *boiling at all*. We
will therefore pass by in silence this
unfruitful epoch. It would be waste
of words to *open our mouths* upon a

---

tities for making a quart of the liquor. Louis
XIV. was so fond of it, that the city of Paris
made him a present every year of a certain number of bottles. A whole pipe of the Hippocras was provided for the famous feast of Arch-
bishop Neville, in 1466.—Vide *Forme of Cury.*

subject where we should find nothing worth *opening them for*. Let us then proceed to the reign of Henry IV., who was long before he had a kitchen of any repute. This monarch, who wished that no Frenchman should be without his *poulet au pot*, at least once a week, had, however, something better than a *poulet au pot* every day himself; and his good wine of Surene was only by way of pleasantry, his favorite beverage.

The Parisians long preserved the poor diet to which he reduced them; and the artists of the kitchen were years before they could pardon him for carrrying off from his sister, *Tonquet la Varenne*, who disgustingly preferred *l'emploi d'ami du Prince* to that of being the cook of an amiable Princess.

Great were the difficulties which Henry IV. had to encounter ! (as one may see in the history of France ;) vast were the projects which he had to accomplish before he could acquire the title of Great, and was enabled to shut the mouths of his numerous enemies !

Whilst he continued to be a Hugonot, he and his followers were often reduced to a very low ebb ; but as soon as he became a *good christian*, he exerted himself more to enable his subjects to put the pot upon *their* fires, than to put it upon *his own*. He was constantly dancing about with his minister Sully, from the *kitchen* to the *scullery*, from the *cellar* to the *garret*, and from the *housekeeper's room* to the *butler's pantry*, to see that every thing was well arranged throughout his dominions. One day, having passed some laws respecting those who were employed in manufacturing vinegar, and who interfered with the compositors of sauces, he immediately founded that interesting corporation of shopkeepers in the city and faubourgs of Paris.

This monarch closed the sixteenth century by renewing the statutes respecting the chiefs of the kitchen, the cooks, the cup-bearers, the confectioners, the pastry-bakers, cake-makers, and wafer-rollers, and began the seventeenth century by establishing a guard to watch lest his gardeners used hog's dung or the sweepings of Paris to manure his grounds. He encouraged Bernard de Palissy to improve the parterre ; and he employed Olivier de

Sorre, the most celebrated man of his day, to ornament the gardens of the Thuilleries with twenty thousand feet of wall.

The Cardinal de Richelieu only just deviated enough from the cookery of Louis XIII., to prevent himself from dying of hunger. Mazarin kept Louis XIV. upon *short commons* during his minority, but the *great monarch* made up for it pretty handsomely afterwards; for the public feasts during the whole of his reign were in a style of splendour and magnificence which has never been surpassed. The *warmest* partisans of those luxuries introduced by this Prince, soon, however, began to shew some degree of *coldness* in their attachments; as ices now for the first time made their

appearance.* When this gallant
monarch ordered particular feasts, as
it was rather his object to make himself beloved than admired, he endeavoured to combine in them every thing
the most delicate and distinguished
that the kitchen could afford.

If the banquets of Louis XV.†

---

* It was towards the end of the year 1660,
that *Procope Souteaux*, a Florentine, introduced
the use of ices at Paris.

† The Parisians erected in a square that bore
the monarch's name, a beautiful statue of Louis
XV. on horseback, supported by the four cardinal virtues: it was executed by Bouchardon,
and destroyed during those scenes of revolutionary
horrors which took place in the years 1793 and 4.
This statue produced the following severe epi-
gram upon the king and Bouchardon.

> Bouchardon est un animal,
> Et son ouvrage fait pitié,
> Il met le vice à cheval
> Et les quatres virtues à pied.

did not equal in splendour those of his predecessor, the little suppers of Louis *the Beloved*, however, surpassed in refinement those of *Louis the Great*. An age of heroes has never failed to be an age of artists : that of Louis XIV. and Louis XV. produced as many of the one as the other. Under these two kings the alimentary art was carried to a point of perfection hitherto unknown to moderns : and the magirologists of France shewed themselves worthy to dispute the palm with those of the ancients. Amongst the most celebrated to whom the pen of the historian has given immortality for their learned works, but whose name the modesty of the author has concealed, we must distinguish the cook of Pierre de la Varonne. This French artist studied with considerable suc-

cess, and like another *Newton*, established a system which has stood the test
of ages, and confirmed to posterity the
true French cookery, whose laws are
to this day universally received, admired, and imitated. *Pierre de Lune*
attempted in vain to eclipse by his
Nouveau Cuisinier, (New Cook) the
productions of his predecessor, but he
had a more dangerous enemy than
Pierre. L. S. R. in his " Art how to
entertain," reproached Varenne most
bitterly for his *Gigot au Laurier*, invented at a period of successive conquests, when nothing would go down
in France but what was laurelled.
We find appearing at different periods
*Le Patissier François, Le Cuisinier
methodique, Le Maitre d' Hotel Cuisinier, L' Ecole parfaite des Officiers
de Bouche,* et *Le Cuisinier royal, et*

bourgeois, of Massialot, who, according to Voltaire, was not of the golden age, when mankind were fed on acorns. *Le Cuisinier moderne*, that which still exists by *Vincent de la Chapelle*, cook to Lord Chesterfield and the Prince of Orange ; * Le *Cuisinier Gascon*, (where every thing is not seasoned with garlic ;) *Le Cuisinier familier*, (for once common ;) *Le Cui-*

---

* The English have translated this work, as indeed most of the other celebrated works of the French kitchen, but often under different names, and without acknowledging their authorities. As it is but common justice that every country should have the merit which is its due, we shall endeavour to restore to France her proper literature, and to recover for her artists an acknowledgment for those divine delicacies, of which the plagiarists of other countries would so unfairly deprive her.

sinier parfait de Menon ; Le Cuisinier instruit, (sometimes learned ;) also of Menon as well as Le Manuel des Officiers de Bouche. *La Science du maitre d'hotel Cuisinier, Les soupées de la cour*, La Cuisine d'office de santé. *La Cuisinière Bourgoise*,* and L'Almanach de Cuisine, (strangled in its birth ;) *Les dons de Comus* of the *Sieur Marin*, given to the public at no small price, together with the *Gabriel Anne Mennier de Querlon*, (a most happy combination ;) *La maison reglée d'Audiger*, better named Maison economique ; *La maison rustique, grande* et *petite*, (always rustic, certainly ;) Le *Manege des changes* of the Sieur *Liger*, (a work by no means

---

* This work also was translated into Italian under the title of *Cuoco Piemontise*.

léger ;) Le Dictionnaire des Aliments
de M. C. D. chief of the kitchen of
* * *, (in which, by the bye, there
is as much about drinking as eating ;)
Le Manuel Alimentaire de *Buchotz,*
(with which it would be difficult to have
a good digestion ;) *La Cuisine et Pat-
tisserie de Santi,* by an officer of health,
*Jourdan de Cointre ; Le Dictionnaire
portatif de Cuisine d'office de distilla-
tion, &c.* The confectionary art boasted
of her own men of science, so skilled in
every branch of the business, that in
attempting to follow them we should
be obliged to exhaust an ocean of
sweets—*Le Traité des Confitures,*
published at the end of the 17th century, was soon buried in oblivion by
Pierre Masson, who gloriously opened the 18th with his *Parfait Limona-
dier.* Jean Goulin, armed with his

confisseur Royal, quickly dashed to the ground the imperfect edifice of *Masson*, and shivered it to pieces like a *wafer*. *Gilliers* and his *Cannamliste* sweetened the residence of the King of Poland, at Nancy, and it only required the two Encyclopedias, Alphabetique, and Methodique, as well as the works of *Dubuissons*, *Macky*, and *Machet*, to prevent him from appearing in the capital of the gormandizing world. If the progress of Ænology* was slower than that of cookery and confectionary, its success, however, was not less brilliant. No sooner had it mounted the *bidet*† and

---

* The science of wines.

† The *Bidet* and the *Rosier* were names successively given to wine coolers in France. Ænology in England is now in a very advanced state

the *rosier*, but it proceeded at its ease, and had its path strewed with roses, where it had been before choked with thorns ; and through which *Gohorry*, *Paulmier*, and *Mysonnier*, had attempted in vain to open an honorable passage. One cannot deny that *Boullay*, *Herbert*, *Colas*, *Bridette*, *Barbaret*, *Beguillet*, *Maupin*, and, lastly, *Chaptal*, and others, have contributed greatly towards the glory of this important part of gastrological science.

Whilst alimentary literature took this high flight in France, neigh-

---

of perfection. We have coolers, *Montief* glasses, and Ravensworth decanters, bearing the names of those noblemen who have attended to their wines. We have also the *argyle* for gravy, and the little *sandwich*, a monument " ære perennius" of the eminent gastrophilist whose skill and ingenuity it records.

bouring nations burned with ambi-
tious desire to mount with the same
lofty wing : but their efforts were not
crowned with full success. Amongst
those men whose pens enlightened the
understandings, and whose pastry delighted the palates of their countrymen, who sought to inspire the people
of Germany, Holland, Denmark, and
Sweden, with a proper taste for good
living, we must notice, prior to the
reign of Louis XIV., *Riffi, Egelnoff,
Bumpolt, Anne Weckerin, Carrick-
ters, Bekonston, Tursten*, and since
that period, *Sachfstedser, Suzanna
Egenin, Sletten, Stalk, Burghart,
Livffi, Paul Iverson*, and *Holdings*.
Amongst the English also, (who were
the great rivals of the French in every
thing, and quickly *trod upon and*

tripped up their heels, whether pur-
suing them over the field of *Mars*, or
revelling at the orgies of Bacchus,)
an innumerable host of heroes and
heroines offer themselves to notice ;
who alternately handled the pen, and
rolled the paste ; who consecrated the
studies of the night to inspire their
countrymen with an elegant taste ; and
the labours of the day to exhibit something more refined than beef-steaks
and mutton-chops, greasy surloins
and leaden plumb puddings.*

---

* In speaking thus of the old English fare, we
by no means intend to hold up these solidities to
contempt: on the contrary, we feel inclined to
congratulate such of our countrymen as can still
afford to make them a part of their Sunday's banquet : but the justice of the historian must not be
biassed by national partialities.

Were, indeed, all the English magirologists who have appeared in the
last two centuries to be drawn up in
battle array, even the accumulated
host which the continent could mus-
ter for ten ages past would be obliged
to fly before so vast an army. We
cannot, however, but blame many who
have concealed their names, and with-
held from us the honour of recording
them amongst the gastrophilanthropists
of the present age. Pardon me, then,
ye divine pillars of the church, and
ye counsellors of the monarch, if your
great modesty prevents my giving to
posterity your illustrious labours, and
recording those who have, at the
smoaking delicacies of a bishop's table or a city feast, composed recipes
for *parish broths*, and *rice soups*, have,
in the plenitude of alimentary hap-

piness, *still remembered the poor !**
But amongst the number of gastrological editors, the name of Samuel
Pegge comes to us as a man whose
apotheosis all the English antiquarian
gastrophilists unite to celebrate.
The † preface which this divine ma-

---

* England is a country, more than any other,
where the noblemen and gentry attend to the
condition of the poor ; and bishops and preben-
daries have invented cheap soups, and ladies and
ladies maids, have cooked them. But if we may
judge from the poor's rate in England, it should
seem, that all this *feeding* only *feeds* the evil.
The *cold* system of Malthus can have no chance
with the *warm* soups of these eminent divines.
Let us hop , however, that the A B C of Dr.
Bell and Lancaster, may aid the general cause,
and that the mental feast may ultimately procure
a corporeal one, without having recourse to
parish soups. and other philanthropic fooleries.

† The title of the book which Dr. Pegge

girological editor gives us to the little
dispensary of the culinary laboratory
of Richard II., is a fountain of gastrological science. The learned writer
commences, as he terms it, *ab ovo ;*
nor is his egg long in hatching, for,
with a profundity of thought which
we cannot too much admire, he observes, that it was unquestionably in
autumn when man was originally
created. That it is agreeable to our
notions of divine benevolence, con-
sistent with every idea that we can
form of God's providence, that our

---

edited is, " The forme of Cury." It may be remarked that the *cury* was a branch of medicine
as well as of culinary art. It is derived from
" *curare*," which signifies in Latin either to
heal, or to dress victuals. This instructive little
work, which contains 190 recipes, was compiled
about the year 1390, by the cooks of Richard I.

first parents should have been placed
in the Garden of Eden, when every
bough was bending with its golden
weight, and every grove presenting a
rich repast for their support.*   How
otherwise, asks this subtle reasoner,
could they have sustained life? they
must have fallen the victims of
famine.   Our gastrological writer hav-

---

* It is curious to observe how different authors
view the same thing in different lights.   Samuel
Pegge, whose mind was wrapped up in gastrological subjects, sees nothing but the feasts of *autumn*
as suitable to the circumstances of the creation.
While Virgil, hurried away by the beauties of
Spring, concludes that that season alone hailed
the infant earth.

Non alios primâ crescentis origine mundi
Illuxisse dies, aliumve habuisse tenorem
Crediderim, ver illud erat, ver magnus agebat
Orbis, &c.—*Virg. Geo.*

ing fully satisfied himself on this simple
point, and, no doubt, at the same time,
all his readers, does not stop long in
Paradise.* He makes no comment
upon the aliments of the antedilu-
vians : he steps over the wide waste
of waters, without throwing any light
upon the diet of the ark, or satisfying
us whether hard biscuit and pickled
pork made a part of their naval stores ;
he passes with rapidity through Lydia
—posts through Greece—barely takes
breath at Rome to pay a visit of com-
pliment to Apicius—and arrives at
once plump in England. Here, after
a short but energetic lamentation over
the diet of our ancestors during the

---

* Although he begins *ab ovo,* he does not proceed *ad mala.* He throws no light on the *mala
mania,* or mad gastrophilism of our first mother.

age of their idolatry,* he launches
forth in their praise, and congratulates
both them and his country for having
received King Gormandus† with open
arms ; and he highly extols the Great
Alfred for having brought back so
powerful a monarch into the bosom of
the church.‡ With a zeal truly religious, Dr. Pegge observes, that the

---

* Dr. Pegge cites Strabo and Cæsar for his authorities.

† Gormandus, or Gormon, was a Danish king :
his capabilities of appetite were such, that gluttons
got from him the appellation of Gormands.—
(Drake. Ebor.) vide Fawkes's Chronology for this
king, epoch. 3, Table 65. This book cannot be
referred to without admiring its excellent arrange-
ment : *but every thing is well arranged at Farn-
ley Hall.*

‡ King Alfred persuaded Gorman to be chris-
tened, when he took the name of Athelstane.

Britons found no difficulty in blending
with their conquerors, and conforming
to the manners of the Normans in
every thing but their temperance;
telling us that in this point they won
over their masters to their own habits
of immoderate eating and drinking;
and as Lord Lyttleton, 1 believe, observes, with an address we cannot but
admire, that the conquered thus re-
conquered their conquerors. How
could this writer have possibly said
with more delicacy or more refinement
of language, that our British ancestors
were by nature theogastrophilists from
time immemorial? or that the climate
of England is one where gastronomy
might be expected to rise with unparalleled vigour and splendid luxu-
riance? Whilst, however, he conveys
thus much in the praise of the Britons,

he by no means refuses to do strict
justice to the Norman kitchen, and
their well founded aversion to great
half roasted pieces of meat. Nor does
he attempt to suppress, that William
the Conqueror had nearly broken his
favorite's jaw for serving him with a
crane swimming in its blood.* After
eulogizing the Norman dynasty, Dr.
Pegge further tells us, that it ceased
only by a great debauch upon the
high seas,† and a noble and royal in-

---

* The name of this favourite, who thus dange-
rously excited his master's irascibility, was Fitz
Osborne. Had the blow not been dexterously
warded off by the King's *dapifer*, who happened
to be present, the poor favourite would unquestionably never have had it in his power to exercise his grinders again.

† The eldest son of Henry I. and his two bro-
thers, were all drowned in a gale of wind in

digestion of lampreys ; a glorious regicide which has immortalized the
lampreys of Lyons.

It is difficult to say, whether the
Norman kings or those of the dynasty
that succeeded maintained the best
table, and laid the most covers.

Richard II. fed daily ten thousand
people. But all these sink into in-
significance before the establishment
of Cassibelan,* who on one occasion

----

crossing from France. They had sacrificed so
largely to Bacchus, that they were unable to ma-
nage the ship, and thus became a sacrifice themselves to Neptune.

* For an account of this king and Lud, (vide
Nig. lib. Edw. 6,) entitled " Ordinances and Regulations for the Government of the Royal Household, &c." Cassibelan or Cassibelanus was one of
the most able chiefs that opposed the invasion of
Cæsar, and combated his passage of the Thames.
(Cæs. bell. Gal.)

H

we are told had forty thousand beeves,
an hundred thousand sheep, thirty thousand bucks and other deer, besides
hares, rabbits, fowls, and all kinds of
game, served up at a single banquet.
Nor was there ever a table served with
more profusion than that of king Lud,
which was covered with smoaking delicacies every day from eight in the
morning till seven at night. Or where
shall we find a Prince of these dy-
nasties to compare with Hardi Canute*
in his Bacchic Martyrdom, who never
flinched his glass till he fell gloriously
under the table, and lay in a state of

---

* Hardie Canute, sometimes Horda Canut, or
Knut, " hard knot"—v. Fawkes's Chronology.—
This king was the first who established four regu-
larly served meals a day, he only reigned about
two years, and died of a drunken bout at Lam-
beth.—(Lib. Nig. dom. Ed. 4.)

insensibility and prostration, till he was borne away *hors de combat*—never to fight again.

Nor can I quit this subject of our gastrological authors without pleading for pardon before the manes of the Rev. Dr. Percy, Bishop of Dromore,* for having omitted to do him justice amongst the writers in this noble science. If any thing can excuse me for an apparent neglect, it must be that this divine Magirologist has confined

---

* The manuscript of the book which Dr Percy edited was written in the year 1512, and bore the title of " Regulations and the Establishment of the Household of Henry Algernon Percy, fifth Earl of Northumberland, &c. The work has always been held in great estimation, and referred to on all subjects of ancient gastrology. It was re-printed in London, in 1770.

his accounts to the dishes that were served, and tells us nothing of the sauces with which they were flavoured. For of what moment is it to us to know that our ancestors fed on birds and beasts, unless we are told by what means they were made inviting to the palate, and salubrious to the stomach ?

As we have already remarked, that the English are a *most thinking nation*, so they seem to have *thought twice* before they could be induced to change the diet of their ancestors, and allow foreign artists to settle amongst them ; but Theogastrophilism has at last prevailed, and the artist of France has established his empire in the British Isles.

In the first years of Henry VIII. neither cabbage, carrots, nor any escu-

lent* root grew in England ; and it has
been remarked that queen Catherine
could not even have a sallad for her dinner till her royal husband had imported
a gardener from the *pays bas.*† Arti-
chokes, apricots, and plumbs appeared
also about the same time. Nor till

---

* Potatoes, the great support of the lower
orders of people, were not known at this period.
They were first introduced into Ireland by Sir
Walter Raleigh, and were said to be brought by a
Captain Hawkins from Sante Fè. Mr. Cobbett,
who often abuses things that are good, has lately
brand d the potatoe with the appellation of the
" root of misery."

† Horticulture had been very little attended to
n England at this period. It however advanced
rapidly in the reign of Elizabeth. The racks and
tortures of the Duke of Alva, drove the gardeners
of the low countries into England in the year
1567, and under their tuition our gardens soon acquired great distination.

after the year 1524 did the turkey*
smoke on the Christmas board, the
carp swim in claret, or hops† add to
the fragrance of *strong October.*

The currant was only brought from
the Isle of Xanthe in 1533, and the

---

* This bird so much admired by every gastrophilist is by some said to be a native of China, by
others of America. It is to be lamented that this
point has not been more thoroughly investigated.
If the cocks be caponized they may be stuffed to
fifty pounds weight.

† Hops were much cultivated in England soon
after their introduction. Thomas Tuffer a lively
poet of the 16th century, who published several
books called " Five Hundred Points of Good
Husbandry," recommends hop planting thus :

" The hop for his profit I thus do exalt,

" It strengtheneth drink and it savoureth malt."
Notwithstanding the partiality of the English for
hops, the Italians consider them as poison, and call
the plant *cativa erba.*

Flemings bestowed the cherry on us in 1540. Notwithstanding the many things which were yet wanting to complete the English kitchen, artists found the means of committing the most glorious regicide known in the gastronomical annals of their history, a history by no means deficient in Regicidical Martyrdom. They fed Henry VIII. to such an enormous size, that he might literally be said to have died of kitchen fat.

His successor Edward VI., although of tender age, shewed a most happy disposition for good eating and drinking ; and often feelingly lamented, that it was his misfortune to be the king of a people, where the alimentary arts were so little advanced. In order to cheer his young mind under this weight of woe, Henry II. sent him an

embassy from France, composed of all
the most scientific gourmands, that his
kingdom could produce. At the head
of them was the Marechal de St. Andro,
a man highly distinguished for his
talent of gustation, and who was ably
seconded in this gastrodiplomatic mission by La Vielleville, indisputably
the first Gastronomist of his age. On
their arrival at London they opened a
table of such exquisite dainties and
such delicate meats, all brought from
France, that the English lords turned
up their eyes with astonishment, and
began to rail at their own climate and
soil for being destitute of such delightful rarities. Nor can we wonder at
their feelings, when we learn that there
were constant relays of twelve horses
each stationed along the roads ; where
they travelled day and night, loaded

with every thing that France could
produce for the supply of the embassador's table. But that which is the
most remarkable in this history, and
what covers with immortal glory the
artists who conducted it, is, that they
so managed their banquets, that neither
beef, mutton nor veal ever appeared,
but to give strength to their soups, and
flavour to their sauces.

In viewing this splendour of the embassador, there is no intention of re-
flecting upon young Edward's hospitality. He did every thing in his
power for their entertainment. His *Mai-
tres d'hotels* had brought them on their
arrival, as an eye witness has assured
us, such substantial fare, that the least
delicate articles served, consisted of
water fowl, and cycnets, which were
instantaneously sent away untouched.

The day being at last fixed for this famous embassy to take leave, they repaired to court, where young Edward appeared like an angel : " velut inter ignes Luna minores," and received them with angelic smiles. The little monarch inquired anxiously if M. de la Vielleville was to remain in London, and on receiving an answer in the negative, the prince seemed sensibly touched at the loss of so perfect a gastrophilist. At the same time recovering himself he requested that the gentleman who was destined to remain at his court might be introduced. As the minister approached him, however, he turned suddenly away, and began conversing apart with Messrs. Gyè and Vielleville, saying in a low tone of voice and laughing, " You will bring me into disgrace with this embassador,

for not finding in my kingdom the
same delicacies as in France, he will
pine and grow thin."; They laughed
heartily at the prince's humour on
looking over their shoulders, and seeing a man of uncommon height, bulk,
and obesity. This gentleman was
called, Renè de Laval, Seigneur de
Bois Dauphin. His size and corpu-
lence were such, that they made it necessary for him to have a coach, and
he was the first Frenchman who
brought that description of carriage
into use. But it was not until the
year 1580 that any coach was seen in
England. The first was introduced by
Arundel, and was drawn by two
horses; in 1619 Buckingham drove
six. Elizabeth appeared at her public
ceremonies mounted on horseback behind her chamberlain, and till after the

third year of her reign, this princess, so magnificent in her retinue, so nice in the adjustments of her toilet, and so splendid in her apparel, (that at her death, Henzner tells us, 3000 different dresses were found in her wardrobe, all of which had adorned her person,) wore nothing but cloth stockings.*

Whatever changes the fashions of Elizabeth's court might undergo, her table underwent none, it remained during her whole reign nearly upon the footing that she found it. Knives† were,

---

* Mrs. Montague, who was tire-woman to Queen Elizabeth, first presented her with a pair of black silk stockings in 1560; and she was so much pleased with them, that after that she never would wear cloth any more.

† Knives were first used in London, 1563, under the auspices of Thomas Mathews of Fleet Bridge. Sheffield was, however, famous for its cutlery in the

however, then first introduced. A picture which Hollingshed gives of the

---

days of Chaucer. So late as just previous to the
French Revolution, there were many tables in
France where no knives were laid : every guest
was obliged to furnish his own. The Revolution
may have made them more common, as during its
sanguinary scenes the people seemed tolerably expert in the use of them. It does not appear, however,
that forks were introduced in England before the
reign of James I. Coryat was the first man who
exhibited them, for which he got the name of
" Furcifer." In the inventory, however, which
Charles V. king of France made of his plate in
1319, a fork is mentioned, but forks were not
common, even in that country at his period. For
many years after they were generally introduced
they had only two prongs, the knife was accordingly made broad and round at the end, and employed to carry the meat and gravy to the mouth,
a practice which the four pronged fork has totally
exploded, and it would now be esteemed such a
mark of ill-breeding, that rather than venture it, the

littleprogress which thearts had made in
the preceding generation, is too strik-
ing to be passed over in silence. There
were very few chimneys, says this
writer, in the large towns. The fire
was, generally made in the corner of
the room, and the smoke found its way
out through the roof, or at the door or
window. The floors were made of
cement, and the house utensils of
wood. The inhabitants slept on straw,
and a faggot made their pillow. Wine
was only to be got at the apothecary's
shop, where it was sold as a drug.

After such a view of the state, we
can form no favourable opinion of the

polished gastrophilist must forego his gravy. An
improvement however might be effected to remedy
this, by having the centre of the four pronged
fork entire, and a little hollowed, so as to prevent
any liquid from escaping.

alimentary art. We accordingly find
that when Elizabeth received embassadors from France, conscious of the
inferiority of her kitchen, she endeavoured to make up by her gracious
manners for the want of more substantial entertainment. One day* when
Messrs de Foix and de Castellan were
dining at her table, she drank to the
health of their king and the queen
mother, and then most graciously sent
them her own cup that they might
pledge her. She at another time pro-
voked Mons. de Sancy to a piece of
very singular gallantry. Luckily she
had to do with a knight of as much
courtesy as intrepidity. After he had
been pressing her with very much
earnestness to espouse Henry IV.

---

* Mem. past, pour servir à l'histoire de France.

" Let us say no more," she replied,
" on that subject, my Gendarme (for
by that appellation she always spoke
of Henry) is not a man for me, nor am
I at all suited to him. Not that I
think myself by any means incapable
of affording a husband every pleasure
he could wish, but I have other rea-
sons, &c."* She at the same time
lifted up her lower garments and shewed more than a leg. Sancy fell upon
his knees and impressed an enraptured
kiss. The Queen was angry at his
presumption, or perhaps feigned to be
so : she alleged that there was a want
of respect in the act. The dexterous

---

* This anecdote of Queen Elizabeth may be
ound in several publications, but particularly in
"Les Memoirs Historiques et Politiques d'Amecol
de la Houssaye, tom. i., p. 78.

Knight, however, quickly did away all appearance of displeasure by saying, " Pardon me, Madam, but if my master himself had been here he would have done the same."

Whilst the Queen of England was thus endeavouring to shine before her court, and with unparalleled effrontery shewed that which ought not to have been shewn, and which she, if she had had any regard for herself, ought above most women to have concealed,* the Queen of Scotland, not less attentive also to the business of the toilet, but

---

* Elizabeth was not very young at this time, and that she had at no period of her life any charms of person, has been generally allowed. Hentzner relates, that when he saw Queen Elizabeth in her 67th year, she wore false red hair, and her bosom uncovered, as was usual with all unmarried women.

much more so to that of the table, modestly concealed what her vanity might have induced her to expose, without any offence to decency. And yet, perhaps, she shewed too much for her own happiness, or for the happiness of those with whom she has been accused of having had nothing to conceal.

The taste of Mary Stewart was highly delicate, notwithstanding she owed her origin to a race somewhat rude till it was ennobled by the table.* Reared in the lap of luxury, an object of general admiration, amidst the flat-

---

* The genealogy of the Stewarts has been ably illustrated by Charles Stewart, Esq. M. P. published in 1798: he commences with Walter, son of Alan, *dapifer* of the King of Scotland, in the 12th century; Mary, therefore, owed her name and her origin to the table.

teries and caresses of a court, at that
time the centre of whatever was polished and refined in Europe, she had eminently acquired every elegant accomplishment and every female grace. It
is no wonder, then, that she quitted
the shores of France with such deep
regret, and shed so many tears at leaving the gay scenes of Parisian mirth,
and the animated halls of festive joy
which every day offered for her amusement. What a contrast did the banquets of her native country exhibit !
what a people for her companions ! we
cannot be surprised at the disgust she
felt, or that she turned away with horror from the *crowdies* and *whisky* of
Scotland, to the inviting *pattèes* and
rossolis of Italy. The man, alas !
with whom she thus regaled, was bar-

barously murdered by her side ; and
the floor of her chamber stained with
his blood, whilst in social converse,
and even in the moment of actual
meal.

Twenty years of imprisonment, and
twenty years of affliction, notwithstanding the severity of the lesson,
were insufficient to correct the natural
levity, or destroy the constitutional
gaiety of her temper : possessed at all
times of vanity, on many occasions it
supplied the place of courage : for in
the chamber of mourning she could
be dissipated, and amidst the preparations for death, she could become
convivial. The end of Mary Stewart
celebrated by a thousand interesting
circumstances, offers one for consideration which shews how well the un-

fortunate queen was versed in festival
manners, and how much also she was
their slave.

When the fatal warrant arrived, and
she found herself at last condemned to
lose her head upon a scaffold, by a
rival who had neither her beauty nor
her address, she sat down at table with
her usual complacency, and having
finished her repast, filled her cup to
the brim, and with a voice as firm as
it was melodious, exclaimed in an
elevated tone :—" Here, my friends,
is to the last moment, that when it
comes my heart may not fail." She
then drank, and called upon her at-
tendants to pledge her. They, ever
ready to shew their obedience and af-
fection, went on their knees, and
mingling tears with their wine, drank
to their mistress.—" Quis talia fando

temperet à lacrymis ?'' Who, though they feel it impossible to admire the unhappy Mary, under the load of crime with which she was, perhaps, but too justly charged, can yet withhold a tear of sorrow for the fate of a queen, or of pity for the failings of a woman ? It seems to have been her principal error, that she mistook the wayward passions of a deluded heart for the sensibilities of a refined nature ; and that yielding to the soft impulse of their dominion, she not only lost sight of every principle of duty, but even outraged every feeling of humanity—Hei mihi qualis erat! Such was Mary Stewart : a woman formed for happiness and society ; who infused mirth and festivity into all around her ; who began life with so many blessings, and who lost them all by so many faults !

* The misfortunes which through many generations overwhelmed the

---

* The illustrious house of Stewart furnishes us with a melancholy example of eleven sovereigns in succession all unfortunate. Robert, the third of his name, and second of it King of Scotland, died of grief in 1406, at seeing his son a prisoner in England; and this son, James I., could not obtain his liberty till he married, 18 years afterwards, an English lady, whose fortune paid his ransom. He was ultimately assassinated in his bed, in the year 1436.—James II. was killed by a canon ball in 1460.—James III., his son, fell in a battle which he lost in 1488.— James IV. had a similar fate in 1513.—James V. died of grief in 1542, at seeing his subjects abandoned to revolt and heresy: and Mary Stewart, his daughter, after a life crowded with misfortunes, perished on a scaffold by order of Queen Elizabeth.—Her son, James VI., who succeeded to the British throne, died certainly in his bed; but he was never esteemed, and had scarcely a friend. His son, Charles I., of England, perished also on a scaffold

house of Stewart, were very unfavourable to the alimentary art in England.
Charles II. had alone paid any attention, and that with difficulty, to the

---

in the midst of his subjects, and before all his
court.—Charles II. led a life of banishment from
his kingdom, sacrificing his honour to his safety.
James II. was dragged with indignation from his
throne, and died in 1720, after having passed a life
in exile, and preserved nothing but the shadow of
a crown.—James III., as he called himself, had
neither kingdom nor subjects. The race is now
extinct. The last of them died receiving private
bounty from the benevolence and charity of
George III. Though we cannot sympathize with
the misfortunes of the latter Stewarts, yet England
is much indebted to their folly, their obstinacy,
and their bigotry, for her civil and religious liber-
ties. It is to be hoped she will long continue to
remember that the same era gave birth to each,
and that if either falls, it is probable that the
other will not long survive !

subject. At his elevation to the
throne, the contrast between the alimentary and the tragic theatre was
truly ludicrous. The first was entirely in the hands of women, the latter exhibited only men. It happened
one evening at the play, that Charles
being impatient for the drawing up of
the curtain, sent to know the cause of
so much delay. The manager waited
upon his majesty in person, and with
due apology excused himself upon the
ground, that *the queen was not yet
shaved!*

Patrick Lamb (a name by no means
ill suited to his part) was amongst the
most distinguished actors in the royal
kitchens during the reign of Charles
II., James II., William and Mary, and
Queen Anne. His book called *Royal*

I

Cookery, contains so many good things that one is not inclined to look much into the works of his predecessors. If amongst the magirological artists and literary gastrologists of the nation, who have run the same glorious career, and have been the most distinguished in the race, we give the following list of names in alphabetical order, it may afford a tolerable coup d'œil of the magnitude of the imposing mass. Bennet, Bradley, Carter Charles, Carter Susanna, Clarke, Leoland Elizabeth, Eales Mary, Frayer, Glasse, Hall, Henderson, Honeywood, Hazlemon, Howard, Jacken Jenks, Lambe May, Macdonald, Mayern, Melroye, Middleton, Murelle, Nott, Perry, Raffold, Salmon, Skeat, Simpson, Smith, Taylor, Wir-

ner, Wooley.* And to these we must
not omit to add Dr. Hunter of York,†

---

* The works of all these learned gastrological
pens might be easily collected, as well as those of
foreign countries, and formed into a complete
Bibliotheca culinaria. Is it not a national shame
that there is not a single profession labouring for
its bread, that has not its distinct library? and
behold! that profession which actually feeds and
supports every other, is left to the mercy of the
wide world.

O vanæ hominum mentes, O pectora cæca!

† There were few things either in physics or
metaphysics that escaped this indefatigable officer of health. Amongst the many instances which
he gave of curious examination into the laws of
nature, he discovered that blades of wheat, when
injured and obstructed in their delivery, *performed* for *themselves* the *Cæsarean operation!*
He gave his observations on this curious subject
to the world in a little pamphlet with illustrative
drawings. The doctor was no accoucheur.

12

a man not more known for his Georgics
than for his renowned *Culina famu-
latrix Medicinæ.* Equally skilled in
agrinomy and gastronomy, in the cul-
tivation of the field, or in the adapta-
tion of its produce; he shone with
unrivalled splendour both in the lus-
trations to Ceres, or at the libations
of Bacchus. Peace to his manes!—
Whatever might have been his own
practice, we cannot bend to that doc-
trine which would make the kitchen
subservient to physic. Nor are we
disposed to yield to him his Ænology
of British wines, with which he proposes to regale us, in preference to
the fragrant Burgundy, or the sparkling Champagne; but we bow down
with this gastrological officer of health
and taste before the brewers of London, when they present us with a pot

of porter in the presence of the best
double Bierre de Mars des Gobelins,
that France ever saw.

If the ages of heroes have been also
those of arts and of learning, they have
likewise been those of amateurs and
connoisseurs. During the reigns of
Louis XIV. and Louis XV., all the
princes of the blood in France, encouraged by the example of their august chief patronized the artists of the
table. The regent in particular contributed greatly to the improvement of
the science. It was under his auspices that the *Cuisine chymique* rose
to notice, and to his exertions, that
its connection with the *Cuisine sca-
vante* was so closely drawn that they
formed only one.

Thus consolidated, it quickly became the rage, nor was there a grandée

in the kingdom, not even Peter the
first himself, who did not delight to
dip their fingers in its sauces ; but
not at the table of the regent, of whose
chemical recipes they had considerable
dread.*

It is in reading what Marmontel
says of the appetite, and the ordinary
habits of this philosophical legislator,
that we may judge if there were many
in a condition to figure away better
than him at the table.—" He dined,"
says this author, " at eleven o'clock,
and supped at eight ; an astonishing
eater and drinker—two bottles of beer,
the same quantity of wine, half a bottle, and sometimes a whole one, of
brandy, at each of his two meals, were

---

* Vide Régence du Duc D'Orleans who was suspected of having dealt a little in poison.

scarcely sufficient for him, without
reckoning the liquors and refreshments
which he swallowed in the intervals."

The Czar, to whom every thing
bowed from the sea of Kamschatka to
the gulph of Finland, who obliged the
son of a simple pastry-cook (Man-
chioff,) to handle the *sword*, as his
father had handled the roller, who at-
tached to his person the principal minister of the most despotic monarch
that ever reigned, and who drew his
naval officers from a country the most
jealous of its freedom.   Yet this com-
manding hero completely failed in an
attempt to establish a colony of a few
oysters on the shores of the Baltic. These
little creatures so delicately formed,*

---

* The oysters of England were in great estimation even in the age of Roman luxury.   The Col-
chester and natives have the preference.

so faithful to their *native beds;* as exquisite in their own taste, as they are
allowed to be to the taste of others,
could never accommodate themselves
to the brackish waters,† which the
Czar had alone to offer for their entertainment. All that were unfortunately plunged into his sea, were quickly
poisoned by the unwholesome beverage, or frozen by his *frightful climate.*
The god of wine, for the most part so
complaisant to the fair sex, was as un-
courteous to the Empresses Anne,
Elizabeth, and Catherine, as the god
of the sea had been to Peter. Not all
the altars which had been reared to
him at the new capital of the empire,

---

* The waters of the Baltic do not contain one
eighth part of the salt of the ocean, and may be
drank without any unpleasant effect.

nor the frequent and copious libations of the *Tartars*, who daily sacrifice at his shrine, could induce the deity to grant them the growth of the vine ; although in some of the southern provinces a few scattered clusters afforded an ordinary liquor.

Catherine, too delicate in her nature to be a glutton, but too refined in her taste not to be choice in her selections, had an Italian artist at the head of her kitchen, who published a work entitled, *L'Apicio Moderno*, which proves that he was not only well acquainted with the French style of cooking, but that he was fully instructed in the delicacies *du Cuisinier moderne François*.

The elector of Brandenbourg, more successful than Peter or his successors on the throne of the Russians, colonized several foreign productions in his kingdoms. The passion of this royal legislator for *great men* and *little turnips* is well known. The latter never failed to be constant guests at his own table, and his neighbours too often found the former guests at theirs.

The decided preference which this literary prince shewed for the French language, the French kitchen and French liqueurs soon established a rich nursery of academicians, artists, and liquorists, at Berlin. The consideration with which the royal philosopher treated them, was such, that he indiscriminately addressed his poems to his professors of science, to the generals of his army, and the artists of his kitchen. His verses to *Noel*, his cook, constitute a perfect master-piece of its kind ; it has immortalized *Noel*

as completely as the smack upon the
breech of Turenne* has immortalized
the name of Master George. One
cannot, however, but lament over the
faded glory of the great Frederic, no
doubt one of the most eminent theogastrophilists that ever filled a throne,
when we learn that on his death bed

---

* The Maerchal de Turenne, breathing the fresh
air one morning at the window, in nothing but his
white dressing jacket, one of his servants, mis-
taking him in this costume for his comrade, Master George, the cook, came gently behind him,
and, with the full force of his arm, gave him a tre-
mendous smack upon the breech. The Marechal,
little accustomed to such mode of salutation,
turned suddenly round, and was astonished at
seeing a man, as if struck by a thunder-bolt, fall
down at his feet, and protest that he had mistaken
him for Master George. Turenne, although
smarting considerably under the rude assault,
only said, ' Well, friend and if it had been Mas er
George, you needed not to have hit so hard."

Rams Hist. of Turenne.

he betrayed unworthy fears lest posterity should rank him amongst those
noble characters whose gormandizing
fame has filled the page of history.
Yet the benevolent gastrophilist will
not judge him too hastily for such
" compunctious visitings," but will
make allowance for the weakness of
human nature in the last moments of
existence. It is besides due to the
royal gourmand to record, that no
such degrading thoughts presented
themselves to his noble imagination,
till the villous coats of his aged stomach, like the tattered tapestry of his
palace, were decayed with service.

But at that fleeting moment they
had lost, alas ! all tone and all elasti-
city, and were ready to desert those
colours, under which they had fought
so many brilliant campaigns, and been

led to so many glorious victories.
Their spirit was then gone, their
strength wasted. The period had arrived when they were no more to be
rallied—they had fled broken and dis-
comfited on every side—the voice of
fame, and the allurements of pleasure,
had alike lost their imposing charms—
all the gaudy scenes of former gran-
deur and delight had vanished; and
the disconsolate monarch was left
abandoned on the field, a prey to un-
availing sorrow, without appetite,
without taste, and without religion !

The Saxons who piqued themselves
upon being the Athenians of Germany,
claimed precedence amongst those artists of the spit, the gridiron, the oven,
and the stove, whose fame for augmenting the delights of the palate, was
best established. But they held in no

estimation the artists of the pen, the pencil, the burin, or the chisel. These were not according with their *taste.* They carried, indeed, their aversion for them to such an extreme, that they swore like troopers against every thing that had the appearance of paper, canvass, copper, or marble, whenever any demands for such things were made upon their purses. And they looked upon their king to be absolutely mad, when informed he had given thirty-thousand Venetian sequins for a Corregio.

It was well for the electors of Saxony, however, that their kitchens were amply furnished and their cellars well stored, or they never would have been crowned by the Dicts and Dictines of Poland.

Noble Poles ! You, before you were

dismembered and divided into three shares like a cake, knew nothing of great and little diets but by name Where is the man, amongst those who boasted of having only made a breakfast of your kingdom, that could have extinguished your gastronomical fame in the days of your corporate integrity ? Where is the man, who would have dared to measure his strength with Staroste Malakowski, whose ordinary draught of liquor was never less than two bottles of wine? Or, where is he who would have ventured to enter the lists with the primate of Poland, who sat at table four days and four nights in succession, drinking indiscriminately wine, beer, mead, and brandy, and that without any intermission of rest, neither losing the

gaiety of his humour, nor experienc-
ing any abatement of his appetite ?

Gaudeant bene nati !

Noble Poles ! is there a man amongst
your devourers, who would order himself to be awakened precisely at mid-
night, without regard to the time he
went to bed, to be presented with a
bucket of hot ale and sugar?   Or is
there one of them who can carry off
three dozen of Hungarian wine from
a sitting, when ten or twelve bottles
only, would lay prostrate the stoutest
Fox-hunter in England, or the wet-
test * double chinned Canon in her
whole Church establishment ?

---

* The author uses this word in the same sense
with Horace, when he says,

———" dicimus *uvidi*

Cum sol oceano subest."—

L. 4. Od. 5.

The Saxons under the reign of their august King of Poland * became as distinguished for their gallantry as for their love of the kitchen. They accordingly invited a number of light heeled artists into their country, to instruct them in the elegant use of their legs, but the artists of the spit agreed so ill with these gentry, that upon every attempt they made to give them a better method of cutting *capers*, they either got a terrible rap on the knuckles, or had their heels tripped up on the spot. But it was very different with the Duke of Wirtemburgh ; for

---

* There is a book with the title of " Saxe Galante," which contains many curious accounts of the feasts which this Prince gave at Dresden. There were three Electors of Saxony, Kings of Poland, in succession, all by the names of Frederic Augustus.

although he was himself esteemed a
man of gallantry, his subjects were
decidedly theogastro-philanthropic.—
There were consequently times when
this Prince did not know very well,
not only upon what leg to dance, but
even upon what leg to stand : for on
one side the women were crying up to
the skies * Noverre, and the pleasures
of a bull, and on the other his subjects
were ringing in his ears,

" *La pause avant la danse.*"

As on a great former contest of this
nature, the members were forced to
yield to the belly, so on this occasion
the paunch carried the day ; and these
troops of skipping gentry who threat-

---

* All the world knows the enormous expense
that this Artist drew the Duke of W. int , and
the representation which his subjects made upon
the occasion.

ened to devour every thing before them,
were driven out of the country like so
many grasshoppers. Vermin, which
by way of parenthesis, having once
foolishly invaded Germany,* met with
their match in a way they little ex-

---

* This account is taken from Les Melanges
d'une Grande Bibliotheque, tom. 20. It is thus
related "In the year 1542, Germany was subject
to a most afflicting scourge. A cloud of locusts
spread over the country and destroyed every thing
before them, those, however, who could bring
themselves to eat them quite fresh and broiled,
found them good and wholesome diet." Locusts
are frequently eaten on the Red Sea, and sailors
navigating it, think themselves fortunate if a
swarm rest upon their rigging. John the Baptist
fed upon locusts* and wild honey; Masconville
when he treats on the locusts, he add , that in his
time they ate silk-worms in Germany, and that
Albert le Grand, had known a girl at Cologne,
who had lived on spiders and snails from the age
of 14, till she died an old woman."

---

* Some suppose that these locusts were beans.

pected. No sooner was the tocsin of
alarm sounded, than men, women, and
children fell upon these devourers, and
completely turned the tables upon
them; as instead of being made the
victims themselves of their devastat-
ing appetites, they treated their little
prisoners after the fashion of St. Law-
rence; or in other words, they indulged
them with a taste of the gridiron, and
then made them contribute towards
the support of that life which they
came to destroy.

In Bavaria the cry was general in
favour of the French kitchen, and effectually drowned the voices of some
Italian artists, who thought to carry
every thing in favour of music *with a
high tone.** Who would believe that

* The Bavarians used to call out, " *Chansons;
Chansons,*" whenever the Italian artists appeared
and these knights of the *Bravura* not understanding

the Germanic body could not meet to deliberate at Ratisbon, without col-lecting with the greatest industry French cooks from every quarter. And that there was a table in the antecham-ber of their hall, covered from morning till night with every delicacy? Nor were strangers visiting the city suffered to pass by, without their Ciceroni, or more humbly speaking their Valet de Place, directing their attention towards these tempting objects. Who is there that must not mourn over the dissolu-tion of such an establishment? Rash and inconsiderate Frenchmen! how many noble institutions have you over-thrown! and how many of your best

---

French very well at first, mistook the term for an expression of encouragement, till experience taught them that it was one of contempt.

artists have lost their bread for this
outrage upon the *German diet !*

Ye Hanseatic towns ! let us not pass
by unnoticed your alimentary fame !
Who is there can cast an eye over
the prostration of your ancient league,
and not heave a sigh for thee, O Hamburgh ! who can behold without indignation, too great for the bile of a
gastrophilist, thy wide and extended
waste of woes ? Thy once hospitable
gates closed against every delicacy !
thy cannon pointed against every inviting charm, every foreign produce !
Thy kitchens, once so savoury that
thou wast esteemed the very *Palais
royal** of Germany, all deserted, all

---

* The Palais Royal at Paris is the principal
residence of the Traiteurs : as Hamburgh grew
opulent, culinary science advanced rapidly. The

desolate! Alas! the Harpies of France
smelt out thy soup kettles,

" Diripiuntque dapes, contactuq; omnia fœdant
" Immundo." ――――

Thy sons enslaved, thy daughters
threatened with the whip—thy patriots
proscribed—thy merchants plundered
—Von Hesse has fled—Parish is driven
from his hospitable domain. And all
thy splendid train of culinary glory is
set like Lucifer to rise no more! Now
mayest thou exclaim as the Dutch did

Schwarz-sauer, and *Weiss-sauer* gave way to the
delicate French sauces; Gastrophilism flourished.
At the season of Leipsic larks, a flight of them
arrived with every carrier to give zest to the
banquets of the merchants. These charming
songsters at " Heaven's gate," are so exquisitely
fat, that they actually melt in the mouth like a
sugar-plumb, they are generally eaten with apple
sauce. O larks, more than ever to be esteemed!

for the amiable and lamented Henry
Hope,

Occidit, occidit,
Spes omnis, et fortuna nostri
Nominis!

In Austria, not improperly called the
Bœotia of Germany, a delicate young
lady will within half an hour after she
has risen from a splendid diplomatic
dinner, (which generally lasts four or
five hours, and where each guest is
presented with at least three score different dishes), devour a plate full of
" *petits poulets frits;*" or after a most
plentiful supper more splendid than
even the dinners, swallow a cup of
chocolate so thick that you may cut it
with a knife, and cram down a load of
pastry besides. Upon a moderate cal-
culation, from thirty to forty thousand
petits poulets frits are consumed every

summer's evening, by these devourers
on the Prater at Vienna. It should
seem as if these feasters never arrived
at that period, when

" Iratum ventrem placaverit esca—"

With them also the adage,

" Regis ad exemplar totus componitur orbis,"

is completely belied. For neither the
sobriety of Maria Theresa, nor the
laws of her son to exclude the wines
of France from his dominions, have
had the least effect in making their
subjects more temperate. Indeed, all
the efforts of sovereigns in these re-
spects are like the labours of the hus-
bandman,

" Naturam expellas fureâ tamen usq; recurrit."

The French Culinœmania raged so
much at Vienna, that the principal

K

topics of enquiry every morning, after
the first salutations had passed, were,
what new graduates had arrived from
the magirological schools of Paris. In
imitation of the ancient Germans,*
nothing of consequence was ever un-
dertaken without a feast. Not a single
little pleasure party was ever planned,
and certainly never executed, where
Champagne and Burgundy did not
flow in rivers. O kitchens of Paris !
O wines of Rheims and Baume, how
much is your country indebted to you !
What services have you often rendered
to France when she appeared on the

---

* Tacitus tells us, that the ancient Germans
never undertook any thing without a feast, and
that those who made the greatest, were always the
most popular, and had the largest number of
followers. The moderns cannot say in this respect—Tempora mutantur !

very brink of ruin ! Where is the man,
who does not remember what prince
Eugene said on the arrival of a minister from Queen Anne, who came to
rescue Louis XIV. from the great
embarrassments that the Succession
War in Spain had occasioned ? After
having spoken of the Marechal de
Tallard, who was at that time a prisoner in England, and observed upon his
insinuating manners, he added, " His
presents of Champagne and Burgundy
to the honourable members of Parliament, who are great lovers of these
wines, have entirely changed the affairs
of Europe."* This great rival of the
great Marlborough, who had more penetration than most men, candidly allowed that the dinners and entertain-

---

* Vide Memoires of Prince Eugène.

ments of Marechal Villars, at the ne-
gotiation of Radstadt, were much
superior to his own. He thus ex-
presses himself, " During the period
that we remained at Radstadt, I gave
balls and suppers, but he (the Marechal) much surpassed me in these
things ; mine were too much in the
German fashion, but I knew no better." What a confession ! We should
be inclined to lament it if, on reading
his verses, the hostility of his views
towards France were not sufficiently
evident. The lines have too much
point not to merit being transcribed :

> " Eugène entrant en campaigne,
> Assuroit d'un air hautain,
> Qu'il iroit droit en campagne,
> Pour y gourmer du bon vin;
> L'Hollandois pour ce voyage,
> Fit apporter son fromage
> Dans Marchienne et dans Denain ;

Mais Villars piqué de gloire,
Leur cria, Messieurs, tout beau:
Pour vous c'est assez de boire,
L'eau bourbeuse de l'Escaut."*

After these acknowledgments of Eugene, no one can doubt of his convic-
tion respecting the power of feasts,
nor that the hardy soldier himself had

---

* That the elegance of these doggrels may not
be entirely lost to the mere English reader, the
Author gives a doggrel imitation :—

Eugène prepared to take the field,
Swore that no force should make him yield,
'Till he had reach'd the Gallic plai,
And quaff'd a glass of good champagne.
The Hollander to live at ease,
Took for his march a store of cheese,
But Villars nobly piqued at last,
Cry'd, " Gently Messieurs, not so fast:
" Scheldt's muddy waters, I should think,
Are good enough for you to drink.

any objection to them. Have we not also upon record, that a French wine even turned a head, that was defended by a triple crown? And did not Petrach express his fears, lest the Pope and the whole sacred college, allured by the juice *des treilles de Baume* should entirely abandon Italy?* Should a con-gress ever be again opened for peace on the Continent, our English embassa-dors, and our Russian allies, (all fine drinkers,) it is to be hoped will be upon their guard against the French-men, " dona ferentes," negotiating

---

* Petrach writing in 1366, to Pope Urban V. in order to persuade him to return to Rome, and stating the different causes which seem to detain the Cardinals on the other side of the mountains, says, I have heard them allege that there is no *wine de bèaume in Italy.*

with wines, and tying the tongues of their opponents.

"Tentatura pedes olim, vincturaque linguam."

We find both in France and in England, that as the alimentary science advanced, and wealth became more generally diffused, many opulent individuals began to rival their superiors in gastronomical refinement. They carried the matter still further, they even disputed the doctrines of science with the most able professors of the age. It is easy to believe, that the sublime discoveries which they made were *seasoned* with the most profound reflections, and expressed in the richest language.

Of late years the advancement of opsartytical knowledge has been so great, that the deliberations of every dinner-table afford the most professed

culinary lecture. There, every thing
is impartially weighed and scientifi-
cally discussed. The abilities of every
actor who makes his debût upon the
alimentary stage is nicely canvassed.
His powers are examined, his taste
criticized, and the rank which he is
calculated to hold duly assigned him.
There is scarcely a noble youth in the
united kingdom now, whose education has been neglected in this essential
branch of science, this first and necessary acquirement of self-preservation.
Whilst we reflect with much satisfaction upon this subject; it is not at the
same time without a mixture of fear,
however, lest in the universal competition that the science excites, and
amid the prevalent rage for national
feasts, the culinary system should undergo some serious revolution. The

triumphs of conquest, and the piety of
the theogastrophilist know no bounds.
The fêtes of Louis XIV. dressed up
every thing *au laurier*, till the laurels
themselves grew sick and faded.   The
miserable club banquet of Vittoria at
Vauxhall was, however, only so far of
the same description that nothing
would go down with the enthusiastic
gourmand but what was heightened
also with laurel sauce.   To see 250
buckets of turtle crowned with bays
was certainly no mean sight; but
against the introduction of a new dish,
such as no artist ever before ventured
to serve, we must enter our protest.
This was nothing less than the *staff* of
a French Mareschal garnished with
such splendid accompaniments, that
although it looked like any thing but
the *staff* of *life*, and seemed to be of

rather crusty materials for royal jaws ;
yet such was the eagerness to get at it,
that princes of the blood, privy counsellors, lords, generals, and admirals,
had in a moment *their mouths full of
it.* Nor did they appear to pay any
regard to the many injuries it had done
to *foreign constitutions*, to the noxious
qualities it possessed, or the numerous
deaths it had occasioned. Much as
we must ever be alive to the prowess
of our arms, and the triumphs of our
country, yet this avidity for *Báton*
dressing seems, " Harpyiis gula digna
rapacibus," and is highly injurious to
the true interests of gastronomy. It is
a vile corruption of taste, and might
lead to a renewal of those savage cus-
toms which our ancestors are said to
have practised in *banqueting upon their
prisoners.*

Ye learned gastrophilists of our two universities ! Ye protectors of science in all its branches ! Why have you no professor of gastronomy ? Is the culinary art of less importance than anatomy and chymistry ? On the contrary, does it not combine both ? The Romans had carving schools* to instruct their youth in the proper dissection of birds and beasts, whilst you confine them, to dissever the limbs of a human body ; and were it not for their own industry and the love of science, they might leave your academic shades to-

---

* These schools, called Pergula, were in the street *Suburra,* which was the *Strand* of Rome. There is an account of them in Pliny, lib. 10, cap. 50.

Also in juvenal,

Cæditur, et tota sonat ulmea cœna Suburrâ.—
                                Sat. 11. l. 141.

tally ignorant of the Doctor Trypherus,* the rise of vapours, the force of
steam, and the due employment of
them in the culinary laboratory.

Besides, learned Sirs, the science is
one which may be of infinite importance in all the objects of life. Your
members, for instance, may ere long go
forth as missionaries to the east, to
rescue the Hindoos from the horrid
obscenities of the Phallic worship, and
save their infatuated widows, not only
from fire in this world, but, as a *fervent*
member of the house of commons†
feelingly exclaimed, from hell-fire in
the next. Now, what arguments can
they use, what means of conversion
can they more effectually employ, than

---

* Trypherus was the master who taught the art
of carving in Rome.—Juvenal, sat. 12. v. 137.

† Mr. W**b**f***e.

by setting before these poor unsophis
ticated rice eaters the superior excel-
lencies of the European kitchen, and
the captivating dainties of christian
diet ?* Even the Persian when he sees
the indefatigable missionary so busy
about the *fire*, may discover some si-
milarity to his own worship, and be
caught in the trap before he is aware
of having at all apostatized from the
worship of his ancestors. " *C'est le
premier pas qui coute.*" Having once
got the young convert into a good dis-

---

* The author knew a Hindoo boy who had
expressed a great desire to become a christian,
and gave as a reason that he might eat pork.
The author believes that this boy is now as good
a christian as if pork had had no instrumentality
in his conversion : he had this account from a very
respectable gentleman who introduced the boy to
him in this country.

position, the rest will be all smooth
and easy.   Amid the descrepancy of
opinions, the instrumentality of gastrology appears to me the surest and
the safest means of conversion.*   But
above all a thorough knowledge of the
alimentary art may be absolutely necessary for those members at home,
who after the fatigues of tutorship look
forward to rustic indolence, and uxo-
rious ease ; who contemplate a happy
retirement to livings annually aug-
mented by the bounty of Parliament,
or to the more solid benefices of their
college liberally bestowed perhaps upon
their curates.   The magnitude of the
first will not be found to do away the

---

* The author hopes that should Messrs. *B.* or
Dr. C. B. cast their eyes on this page, it may
obviate many difficulties.

necessity of culinary art and domestic economy, though the surplus of the latter may possibly leave them no means to call it into practice.

Ye learned body ! despise not these hints which I have ventured to throw out with all due humility at the close of this history. If any of you are in-clined to quarrel with the justice of the legislature, you will do well to recollect " *half a loaf is better than no bread,*" and that the ingenuity so many ex-cellent financiers have shewn in taking from *Peter to pay Paul* is neither new nor uncommon. Were I to hazard any advice it might now be deemed no better than " *moutarde apres diner.*" And yet, " *stricto pane tacetis ?*" It may be worthy of reflection, that as the honourable house has got its *finger in the pye,* it may soon think that the old dynasty of tithes has reigned long enough, and leave you no bread with your Living, justly concluding that the " living bread" will last you to all eternity.

FINIS.

J. GILLET, Printer, Crown Court, Fleet Street.

For EU product safety concerns, contact us at Calle de José Abascal, 56–1°,
28003 Madrid, Spain or eugpsr@cambridge.org.

www.ingramcontent.com/pod-product-compliance
Ingram Content Group UK Ltd.
Pitfield, Milton Keynes, MK11 3LW, UK
UKHW010336140625
459647UK00010B/644